I0058354

An Entrepreneur in Asia

A Personal Journey
of Global Proportions

By
Irl M. Davis

An Entrepreneur in Asia

A Personal Journey of Global Proportions

Copyright © 2005 by Irl Michael Davis

All rights reserved. No Part of this book may be used or reproduced by any means, graphic, electronic or mechanical, including photocopying, recording, taping or by any information storage retrieved system without the written permission of the publisher except in the case of brief quotations embodied in critical articles and reviews.

Global One Productions, LLC

EAN-13: 978-0-9890839-0-4

Printed in the United States of America

All rights reserved.

ISBN-10: 098908390X

Library of Congress Control Number: 2013934377
CreateSpace Independent Publishing Platform
North Charleston, South Carolina

A Must-Read Guide for Every Businessperson Wanting to Expand to the International Marketplace!

To my Mother, Orlena, who gave me compassion.
To my Father, Irl, who gave me the entrepreneurial drive.
To my Sister, Sharon, who gave me determination.
To my daughters, Dea and Molly, who gave me their devotion.
To Carolyn, who gave me her unwavering Love.
To each of you, I am eternally grateful.

Acknowledgments

This has been an exciting ride. If it hadn't been for a devoted group of dedicated people, my inspiration would still find me back at Chapter 1.

My thanks to Rusty Fischer, who provided the encouragement to continue writing. I would like to acknowledge Dezan Shira, Ltd. for their help and support of my company in China. They are an excellent example of a professional resource for the businessperson. They can be contacted at www.dezshira.com.

The people portrayed in this book are fictitious. They are representative of my 30 years of experience and are merely a display of my opinions. Any resemblance to any person is only purely coincidental.

Specific facts were obtained from public domain data banks available on the Internet and from Dezan Shira's book, *China Briefing*, also available on the Internet.

CONTENTS

ABOUT THE AUTHOR

IRL "MIKE" DAVIS was the founder and CEO/ President of A/D Electronics, Inc. and A/D Electronics Hong Kong, Ltd. Established in 1984, these companies sold and distributed electronics components throughout North America. Both companies were sold in 2005. Mr. Davis presently works as a consultant helping others to be competitive in the global markets.

Mr. Davis was born on a ranch in north central Oregon where he established his first business at the age of 13. The summer business allowed him to finish college and begin his career in corporate America. Between 1971 and 1984 Mr. Davis traveled throughout the USA, Europe, and Central and South America giving him the experience to establish his own company in 1984. By the year 2003, Mr. Davis had conducted business in Vietnam, Taiwan, China, Hong Kong, South Korea, Japan, Singapore, Malaysia, Mexico, Philippines, and Russia.

Mr. Davis holds a degree in Electrical Engineering and has conducted business in over 15 different countries. Mr. Davis has over 30 years experience in Manufacturing, Operations, Supply Chain, Marketing and extensive experience in China, Eastern Europe and the Middle East. Mr. Davis has created and managed manufacturing facilities and distribution locations throughout Asia. In addition he has marketed and sold electronic products and his consulting services in over 17 different countries. Companies call him when they need to develop strategies in emerging markets, creating manufacturing supply chains and to develop global business strategies. He offers a unique combination of Engineering Management,

Law, International Business and Strategic Planning. Highlights of his career include: Appointed as a Washington State Trade Representative (2008) and assisted with the development and implementation of international trade, goodwill, and diplomatic efforts in cooperation with the office of Lieutenant Governor for the State of Washington. Appointed by the Washington State Governor to serve on the Global Competitiveness Council. The council was convened by the Governor to identify ways to enhance Washington's competitiveness in the world marketplace and to help frame the future for Washington. In 2010 Mr. Davis submitted a Patent related to lasers and their portable applications. He was awarded the "Marco Polo" award in 2005 for global success in International business. In 2008 – 2010 he held the position of USA Representative of ISPAT, the Investment & Support Agency of Turkey, that reported directly to the Prime Minister of Turkey. Mr. Davis' specialties include: Cross Cultural Negotiations, Foreign Manufacturing, Sourcing, Logistics, International business relationships, Chinese Business Law and Global Business Strategies.

Mr. Davis makes his home in the State of Oregon and can be contacted via email at: irld@globalaonepro.com

Why Read This Book

*"What is happening in Asia is by far
the most important development in the world today. Nothing else
comes close…for the entire planet.
The modernization of Asia will forever reshape the world as we
move toward the next millennium."*

~ John Naisbitt,
Megatrends Asia

- Are you planning to expand internationally?

- Do you feel that to remain competitive in today's market-place you must transfer your manufacturing operations to a foreign country?

- Are you considering expanding your product lines to some of the fastest growing economies in the world?

If you answered "Yes" to one or all of the above questions, then founder and CEO of A/D Electronics Hong Kong, Ltd. Irl Davis has the book for you. ***An Entrepreneur in Asia:*** *A Personal Journey of Global Proportions* is a must-read guide for every businessperson wanting to expand to the international marketplace!

Why *An Entrepreneur in Asia*? Consider the following: China is currently the fastest growing consumer economy in Asia and it is the second largest *world* economy. (That's no typo: the second largest *world* economy.)

In addition to China, other Asian economies are continuing to grow and expand their manufacturing operations. Collectively, the Southeast Asian region offers a population of over 250 million consumers, workers, and managers and is continuing to grow despite the current world economic slowdown. Most Asian governments are stable and pro-business and all are actively seeking foreign investment from companies like yours.

But how do you go about it? How do you wrangle the proper paperwork, travel time, cultural differences, language barriers, and political land mines that are inherent in doing business overseas?

Who do you turn to for help? Who can you trust in a foreign land? Look no further: Irl Davis has been there, done that, and now he shares his expertise in his new book, *An Entrepreneur in Asia*.

An Entrepreneur in Asia also shares with readers the local customs that might trip them up if they're not properly informed, and contains numerous personal anecdotes that are written in Irl Davis's folksy, occasionally hilarious, no nonsense style.

Isn't it time you considered doing business in Asia?

When you do, *An Entrepreneur in Asia* is your guidebook …

INTRODUCTION

As we can clearly see, the world is changing and the accessibility of new world markets is becoming available to small business owners. Not only are they becoming accessible, it's becoming necessary to our own survival and we must participate if we are to survive and, indeed, flourish. Never before have we seen such an expanding market and never before have we seen so many competitors try to capture it.

World trade and globalization is no longer for the large multinational companies, it has opened up for the small to medium size companies as well. It has not only opened up, but we must begin to compete within this vast arena if we are to survive.

Learning from someone else's experiences is the most direct way to understanding what to expect. This book is based upon some of my early experiences that might find some relevant impact on your business. If you are considering entering the global market or have already begun your own journey (there's that word again!), this book might help you to consider modifying your behavior enough to achieve your goals.

Several years ago I was sitting in Shanghai talking to a few government officials about the emerging businesses around the area. I was told that their statistics showed I was one of the few (in the 1% category) foreign businesses who did not take on a Chinese partner but forged ahead by myself as a true wholly foreign owned company/organization.

I merely smiled and didn't tell them that in my early career this bold move wasn't necessarily by design, but one of necessity (i.e. lack of funds).

Along the way in this two-decade journey there have been some eye opening experiences that I wanted to share with the emerging global businessperson; I do that now. The number of markets they serve will distinguish the new business in the 21st Century by its capability and not necessarily by the market.

Globalization will change the nature of opportunity and competition. It's the intent of this book to help the businessperson capture this opportunity, and with that said I think it's just about time to start this journey.

Are you ready???

If so, let's take that brave first step together ...

THE JOURNEY 1

I struggled long and hard with what to title the Introduction to this book. I don't often do that. In my business, decisions come hard and fast and, once you make them, you stick with them. (Sound familiar?)

But a book? Man, that's forever! I knew something dry and subtle wouldn't do; this isn't a textbook and I don't want you pulling out dictionaries and thesauruses in order to get the most out of it.

Something irreverent and whimsical wouldn't do, either. (Although I admit I was sorely tempted to get out my handy, dog-eared copy of *1,001 Jokes for Book Introduction Writers!*)

So I took the "less is more" route and called it, simply, "The Journey." Because, in the end, that's REALLY what this book is all about. Not just the physical journey you, a colleague, or even your company might one day make to Asia. Oh, it's that, but it's so much more, in addition.

This book is about the personal journey you're on right now. Chances are you bought this book because your company is at a crossroads: To expand or shrink; change or fail; move forward or fall behind.

The very fact that you bought a book with "Asia" in the title means you're aware of the globalization trend and are eager, or at least envious, to keep up with it. But how? How do you go about it? What tools will you need? How will you, and your company, change? What will we both be like 1 year from now? 5 years?

10 years?!?

What, really, is my first step?

I can't answer all of those questions; of course, no author can. (Unless you're writing your autobiography, that is!) But what I *can* tell you is this: No matter what path you take, no matter what country you and your company "invade," no matter what your next step is, you can't begin without first taking some kind of a journey.

It may be, at this point, as simple as a journey of information. Finding resources, looking up Websites, subscribing to a magazine that caters to global entrepreneurs. It may be a physical journey, to China, to Taiwan, or to some of the other countries I detail in the Table of Contents.

It may even be a philosophical journey, a smattering of "what if" questions and "maybe this" possibilities rose at your next board meeting, a copy of this book in front of every employee.

More than likely, it will be a personal journey.

I hope I can help ...

My Personal Journey

My journey began with a simple realization: The movement of the marketplace toward globalization is like a giant jigsaw puzzle and, for today's most successful businesses; the pieces are finally coming together.

As more and more companies attempt to understand how the global puzzle works, however, they may not be able to keep up with the requirements of real-world fieldwork unless their leaders and employees understand what happens outside their offices and how to create a truly global business.

Hopefully, that's where I come in: When I first stepped off an airplane into my first foreign country it was exhilarating, exciting, adventurous, and intimidating all at the same time. Filled with anticipation and anxious doubts, I began my international business travels in the early 1970's.

Those were heady days for my foundling company, and me and oftentimes I flew by the seat of my pants, but at least I was flying. There were few, if any, books like this available back then; in many ways, though it would be years, decades even, before I finally put pen to paper, I was already writing my own guidebook to doing business in foreign countries.

Years later, armed with a decade of experience and an eye for the future wave, my Asian business ventures began during the early 1980's. I might as well have been one half of Lewis & Clark: To see another western face in rural China during those times was a rare occurrence, indeed.

Not only was it a journey of global proportions, and one made, for the most part, alone, but it was likewise a journey of knowledge, education, and business acumen. As a result, basic concepts of building relationships and trust beyond our cultural borders became a critical element in my success.

Along the way, there have been lessons both amusing as well as ones that filled me full of anxiety. (Don't worry; you're about to read about most of them and, hopefully, enjoy more of the former and avoid some of the latter.)

My personal, global journey through Asia was filled with episodes of laughter, delight, business success, project failures and wonderful friendships that, I'm glad to say, continue to this day.

You might be wondering why I wrote this book, and I'll admit it wasn't an entirely voluntary act. Writing this book about my journeys in Asia was stimulated by a number of people asking questions.

These questions came from people in businesses that are just starting their journey to students who are curious and fascinated by entrepreneurship, and after hearing the same questions over and over again I agreed with them: Someone ought to write a book.

GLOBAL FRONTIERS

The New Wild West?

I consider today's budding sense of entrepreneurship to be very reminiscent of the pioneers of the old American Wild West. Expanding to reach other markets to better their company, themselves and their family, today's new settlers may have traded in covered wagons and beef jerky for plane tickets and laptops, but the adventurous sense of spirit is still the same.

As products and services saturate our existing markets we are either faced with extinction or we must step up to the competition and join the expanding global entrepreneur.

Look around you; chances are the signs are already everywhere you look.

When I started my company, it was in the basement of my home and I was by myself. I had borrowed money from my parents, mortgaged my home, and floated money on my credit cards (not a practice I would suggest, by the way). In retrospect it sounds exciting, brash, and bold, but at the time it was downright scary.

Still, I had a vision that needed to be seen through to fruition and, to do this day, I'm proud that my idea was one born out of need; not greed. My particular entrepreneurial idea was based upon a single vision that offering cost effective products to my customers, along with an exceptional support/service support program, would be a winning combination.

What happened, in fact, was that I shortened the customers' supply chain, thereby moving them closer to the raw materials they needed and, in the process, decreasing their cost all the while increasing their control. This, coupled, with my desire to build close relationships with my customers AND my suppliers helped move my business from a startup operation to a thriving endeavor.

It wasn't just pluck and hard work that got me out of the basement and into the boardroom, though: Closely held relationships were the single most important key that opened this particular door for me.

In reflection, it was first realized that we had an opportunity because our customers were willing to give us orders based upon our ability to provide cost effective products. Simply put, we were fairly good salesmen. However, good salesmanship is only the first step (although a critical one). If you cannot obtain an order (get a contract or some form of agreement with someone that will give you money in exchange for a product or service) everything you do is just "tourism."

I won't go into global salesmanship here (as that could be another book; hey, *there's* an idea). However, unless you can prove to yourself that you can get an order stateside, why waste your time and money expanding into a global territory? As my old college professor used to say, "Don't put the cart before the horse." You must be assured that you can sell (and achieve the golden order) before putting your house up for mortgage and starting a business, global or otherwise.

During the early days, our relationships with our customers (and potential customers) enabled us to expand into other countries. Our open trust with each other gave us the necessary flexibility to experiment in shortening the supply chain for them, which in turn translated into the secret of our success.

There were other secrets in my future: I learned quickly that what worked stateside didn't always work abroad. There were subtle lessons to be learned, mistakes to be made, and knowledge to be gained in almost every foreign business transaction I made.

Appreciation for cultural differences and interest in cross-cultural history helped me develop a sensitivity to different business techniques – often ranging from country to country – and allowed me to integrate them into my ability to get things done in a foreign land.

I believe that experience provides the best teacher. Along the way, reading, finding a mentor, and obtaining formal (academic) training certainly helps. However, this work is only designed to prepare you for stepping into the actual, real world events that will transpire and that will most certainly require your attention. You may only *want* to get your hands dirty, but step into it you *must*.

My personal journey began with me literally "stepping into" Asia and developing a global business from the ground up. Some of these experiences I am sharing with the reader in hopes that they will learn, laugh, and become less anxious about what will happen when they finally step off that plane and begin their own personal journey.

I know we're all busy, and that some countries are more appealing to us than others. But as you begin this book, I would suggest that you read all the chapters, as there are parts in the section on "Korea," for instance, that you will be able to apply in other countries, and vice versa. Not only that, but by reading about the cultural sensitivities of these specific countries you will eventually realize how important they are to all countries, in Asia and beyond.

I have separated the experiences about Expats from the countries themselves, as this is a section you may want to come back to and review after a few months of fieldwork have provided you with enough of your own personal experiences to make the chapter even more relevant. This section in an important one for *any* businessperson considering hiring an Expat for *any* country, let alone the ones I've chosen to profile on the following pages.

Be forewarned as you begin your research: The availability of information on globalization is vast, and getting vaster all the time. No matter how serious you are about expanding overseas, it's easy to see that globalization is a popular subject and a serious consideration for the modern businessperson.

My approach to this "information ocean" – obviously this isn't the only book about doing business overseas to ever be written – is to provide stories about my actual, real-life experiences. Why? I hope that by leading with real life examples it will help the reader in preparing them for their first or second step into expanding their business, even as it helps put the information I'm providing along the way into proper perspective.

Before entering into my experiences, however, it is important to understand the perception of globalization and what it really means to you as *An Entrepreneur*.

WHAT IS GLOBALIZATION?

I am amazed how much we use the word "globalization" within our vocabulary, and yet how few of us really absorb the true meaning of the word even as we toss it around so frequently.

The 21st Century has brought this buzzword into the inventory of the most overused and least understood words in our vocabulary. The problem is that most people (commentators are usually the biggest culprit) do not appear to have enough of an understanding of elemental economics to use the word properly. Actually, I find that most people are usually fixed on the political and social issues of their nation – state, versus the economic ones. But isn't that where we, as businesspeople, should be putting most of our focus?

To better understand the concepts at the heart of true globalization, it is important to look further at this exchange (economic; and why commodities flow as we think they do). While on the national stage, it is politically "reasonable" to view globalization on a national-social perspective.

I argue against this mindset, however, as there really is no connection between nation-states and the economic entities within the nation. I can already hear a roar of arguments coming from that statement, but I think you can find discussions on this topic within the halls (and mothballs) of the old libraries and halls of academia, so it's certainly not a new or unique topic of discussion. (Or, for that matter, argument.) I argue that economic exchanges take place between companies (organizations) rather than nations or groups of nation-states.

Globalization is not just about trade. It's about allocation of resources. You cannot measure globalization in statistics or the growth of an international business. It is not just about marketing and selling in other parts of the world (therefore not restricted to its statistics).

If this is true, then what the heck *is* "globalization?"

To help give us a clue as to how to define this term, let's take the issues of international trade "theory" and trade "policy." The first discusses the policy around the exchange of "stuff" (which could be services, products or just an exchange of ideas) and the second discusses the policy around what is perceived to be reasons based upon social or political concerns (i.e. political policies).

Remember back in our old classes on economics? Maybe even as far back as Economics 101? Pure economics have no moral or social dimension. If they do, then they fall into social-political policies and are not economic (although it is true they can affect them).

Let's stay on track: Globalization is about developing a company's skill to utilize world resources to meet world customer demand (and to do this profitably) without regard to its location.

Simply put, it's about positioning your company so it can choose any market. However, it's really not about marketing and selling at all. It's really about obtaining and increasing the company's competency to be profitable. This is why globalization is not restricted to the big companies.

It's for everyone.

And it's why small businesses like yours and mine must "globalize" to stay alive.

WHAT GETS IN THE WAY?

If we look at the purpose behind GATT and the WTO, it is essentially to "reduce physical and administrative barriers to international trade."[1] However, if we look carefully they are actually setup to prevent rational economic growth rather than to help them out. Why? Remember "pure" economics: It's not about social fairness or equal opportunity.

I certainly am not saying it's not important; I just want to ensure that the reader understands the full purpose of social-political organizations of nations and why they affect your company, in particular, and all companies, in general.

---

1   Russell G., China (WTCT, Tacoma, Washington) 2003

I personally and enthusiastically believe in equal opportunity and social fairness. However, we must acknowledge such philosophical luxuries come with a price tag. Good business economics looks at everything as factors in assets (including societies, nation-states, individuals, etc.).

The key is to obtain a "balance." The WTO and GATT have an opportunity to create a world where there are no borders, but their real challenge will be to manage the negative social effects of progress while doing so.

Now, let's extend this a bit farther: Another factor that gets in the way of this discussion of "pure" economics is the country's culture, history, and individual beliefs, along with the political climate of the country of your choice. This "baggage" is easily doubled when you take into account your own beliefs, your own culture, and your county's political climate. (Wow, that's A LOT of baggage!)

It is important to know that in today's (and tomorrow's) requirements to be a successful entrepreneur require that you not only approach certain challenges, but in fact you must bridge *all* of these challenges.

THE GLOBAL ENTREPRENEUR

Globalization brings about changes in the activities of the "manager" and it also changes the requirement of "management" itself. I believe that the procedural based management systems (if I am faced with "a" then I do "b" – thus follow the procedures based upon historical or "proven" procedures) must change due to the demands of globalization.

The new system must be more individual-empowered and also become based upon cross cultural performance. For example, you cannot impose sales targets based (or defined) upon a national statistic or national learned procedure. In other words, you cannot act upon these facets with a nationality mind set (set performance criteria based upon national knowledge, etc.).

This is merely a lot of words to say that you cannot think as a "Frenchman" or an "American" when considering globalization. You must think as a "global manager" and no longer manage your company as a "French" company or "American" company (or whatever country in which you happen to reside).

In order to be globally successful, you can no longer think in terms of a "French" market or an "American" market. You cannot think in terms of product types or countries, but must think only in terms of the customer. The supply chain must now be thought of as the market segment. This is a huge statement for change when considering how we think today, but it's at the heart of globalization and it's something you must get used to as the future marches ever onward, with or without you.

A lot of previously successful entrepreneurs are "going global" only to find themselves succumbing to frustration and failure. While talking to my friends in Beijing, for instance, they find that 89% of foreign businesses attempting to establish a foothold in China fail due to the lack of cultural understanding and/or understanding of the "Chinese system of doing business."

So what is the lesson to take away from this discussion? No longer can we demand that the way we are presently doing business is the way you will continue, especially with all of the unique and uncontrollable factors expanding into a foreign country bring to the table.

As we move into the depths of the 21st Century we will have no choice if we want to succeed in the new business world. But first, let's take that initial step …

A Step into the Future:

Video Conferencing & Beyond

One of the leading causes of our accelerated "globalization" is the Information Technology, or IT, transformation we are all currently undergoing. How we communicate has been evolving quickly, to say the least, and even *that* is an understatement.

During the early 1970's Xerox Corporation was a leader (if not the only company at the time) in communication technology. I remember the early forerunner to the fax machines – it was called the Telecopier. It would transmit a document in, get this, less than 3-minutes! At the time, this truly was a remarkable device. The only problem was that it needed the same device on the other end of the phone line.

By the time I began my business, the only way to effectively communicate with the factories in Asia was with a Telex machine. This was a device that you would type your message and at the same time it would punch holes onto an inch-wide paper tape. Then, you would insert this paper tape in a "reader" and dial the other telex machine. It would then transmit this "document" and automatically typed the message on the distant machine.

By the mid 1980's the technology of the telecopier transformed into what we now know as the fax machine. This particular adaptation literally transformed my business overnight. For instance, we could now draw pictures of what we could not say over the phone or telex machine, such as of a product or a concept, which are much easier to visualize than to verbalize. (Especially when verbalizing meant translating hundreds of tiny hole punches.)

Suddenly, we could communicate without knowing the language, dialect, or customs of the person on the other end of that phone line. In no time, thanks to one item of technology, our business doubled.

Likewise, I feel that we are on the steps of another new transformation in communication across countries, cultures, and language. Video conferencing, I believe, will do for modern companies what the fax did 20 years ago. Yes, video conferencing is already available, but only at a very high cost and to large budget companies. There have been steps in video conferencing that are obtainable by the small business person. Apple computer and its iSight product is one example of these devices.

As this technology improves we will be able to hold up a product and have live discussions with R&D departments around the world. We will be able to participate, in real time, during team meetings while each team member might be in another country.

The impact of video conferencing to the small global business will be substantial, to say the least. It will resemble what the fax machine did for my company, (and hopefully with the same economic results). Improved communication across cultural borders, in real time, will be the competitive key to future success.

As we all know, the Internet has changed the way we obtain information and (once again) changed the way we communicate: Now we can have live conversations over the internet (Instant Messaging, iChat, Yahoo, etc.).

There are thousands of books written on this communication revolution, but as with this book: real life wins out over theory every time. Never before has the availability of information been so accessible, nor the need to master it so crucial.

This momentum will move video conferencing from the mere realm of science fiction into a viable means of communicating with people on the other side of the world. Today, I have seen small businessmen talk with their staff using Apple's revolutionary iChat. Using the Internet, the cost is small; the rewards can be huge.

This affordable computing power is leveling the playing field. Not too many years ago it was only available to companies with lots of cash. Today, the small businessperson can now compete with others within this global market.

Regardless of the technology, however, the basic question will remain: How do we satisfy the customers who now have global choices?

There is no longer a perceived trade off between price and quality. Globalization now offers better arrangements for the customer. Information Technology is the "skin" which holds all of this together.

Today, we are faced with better information and better informed customers that have better choices. All of this places a huge mirror in front of us and asks us the question: What is our true value?

I foresee an end to the trade-based chain. A trade-based chain has a middleman importing, another holds stock, and another could even be selling the product. Each organization is marking up the product before the customer buys.

The infusion of Information Technology and knowledge is demanding better resource utilization. The systems between the supplier (prime) and the final customer will be better utilized. The systems will be integrated and interactive. It will become a supply-demand system.

All of this leads us to become a very agile organization. This means we must utilize all assets (including networks, webs, people and other organizations). The successful organization will shorten the supply-chain for their customers. In doing this, we become more competitive.

YOUR NEW COMPANY PROFILE

It is important to see the new requirements to be a successful company in the 21st century before we implement them. It is also becoming more obvious that managers will need to remove themselves from national allegiances, especially when we begin changing past practices and start integrating new processes that are rapidly emerging. The shift to "globalization" opens up markets for everyone, but it also opens up these markets to more competitors. As a result, the market becomes fluid, the pace becomes hectic, the competition stiff.

How will we respond?

It is becoming more important to create a "supply-chain" driven company rather than a market reactionary one. Let's explore this a little further: Just last year I sat down with one of my major customers. My company was becoming very integrated with their processes, and as a result the relationship we had with one another was quickly evolving.

We even created our own warehouse facility within their global organization, thereby taking full responsibility of global shipping, logistics, inventory, etc. Basically, we shortened the supply-chain of this customer from the raw material to their factory floor. The customer no longer worked with three different companies – one for warehousing, one for transportation, and one for manufacturing the parts.

During the past few years we eliminated three steps (eliminated other companies doing service work within the supply-chain) reducing the cost by 40%. During our meeting the V.P of Material demanded we reduce the cost an additional 10% per year. Asking him what might happen when the cost reduction became lower than the cost of material, he replied that "we will pay him to take our product!" Even though all of us were laughing, this very common story illustrates the supply-chain evolution that is changing how we do business today.

This is why the 21st Century company will be distinguished by its capabilities. It will be rewarded with new customers by the reduction of supply-chain steps. Therefore, classic marketing and sales strategies, techniques, and practices will not be enough for the new small business entrepreneur. Your competitiveness will depend on your supply chains.

Why is this? Well, part of the reason is that in today's business world (business-to-business, or B2B) the customer base is well-informed. Actually, it can even analyze where the value is created. Therefore, to compete in this world we must base our product (or service) on the efficiency of the complete supply-chain.

To give an example of this, let me share with you an example of outsourcing a product that I recently completed. I do not fabricate the product in my own manufacturing facility. The sub assemblies come from other global locations that are more efficient with R&D, engineering design, and complex assembly. With the availability of IT (video conferencing, etc) the coordination was fairly straightforward. One part of the product was manufactured in Russia, another in China, another in the USA, with final assembly in Mexico while calibration and packaging was conducted in market centers around the world.

Talking to a number of companies, it has become apparent that few companies accept that effective performance in the global economy will include a radical change in the attitude required for its survival, let alone obtaining competitive success.

How does one start? The beginning is to abandon one's own national-based mode of thought and move toward considering the business domain (or the complete environment in which you conduct business) in which you operate. A business can no longer consider "the Asian Market" or the "South American Market," but instead must consider their market to be borderless and your product/services supply-chain flowing across these borderless areas.

Marketing to this new era of businesses will require a radical perspective alteration. The businessperson must direct his attention to where value added conversion actually takes place and what constitutes value within your customer's mind. No longer can we do business at arm's length; we must now develop a collaborative relationship, no matter what the distance between us. (Remember, new technology will soon make physical distance a moot point.)

It is no longer good enough to build a brand and promote it. The buyer in our new century is more complex and knows where value is created. To survive in this new dimension, we must appeal to the experience required by these emerging companies and adapt accordingly.

Thus high value work gets done where intellectual capital is available (such as in the highly developed world), and the manufacturing/assembly of parts gets done where there is accessibility of raw materials and where the physical labor is favorably accessed (as evidenced in the low-cost, developing world). As managers we must modify our view about the emerging reality of business and not its past practices.

It's called the future; it's here now.

CHINA – A LAND OF MYSTERY, MAJESTY AND... MONEY! 2

If everything you know about China comes from reading the placemats at your favorite Chinese restaurant, I'd like to invite you on a magical, mystical journey into a land where, one day soon, you just might find yourself doing business.

It's a land filled with opportunity, hope, culture, history, and charm, and if you think it's someplace a little too complicated, foreign, or archaic in which to do your business, I'd like to ask you to reconsider your opinion.

A recent study indicated that the current growth rate, if maintained, would put the Chinese economy bigger than that of Japan and the United States in the year 2020. Now if that's not an incentive to invest in a few Berlitz tapes and learn a phrase or two in Chinese, I don't know what is!

But let's not just rely on facts and figures to prove my point. I would like to give you *my* experience in China to date and share some thoughts for the future of the often mysterious China.

Keep in mind that when we talk about issues in America and China, there are usually two sides of each coin. Experts say that doing business in Russia is like rolling the dice; there are six sides to each of their coins.

Well, if Russian dice have six sides then in China they have seven: Six sides you can discover but the seventh you never will see. But if China keeps some of its mysteries to itself, there is still plenty of business to go around and an ever-growing population with ever-expanding wallets is always in need of something else to buy.

Could it just be what you have to sell?

The other fact of life we need to remember is that Chinese culture is very different than our own. Specifically, they are accustomed to a powerful central government. Whenever I was asked about the changes in China I have advised them not to follow our model of democracy, but to develop their own that can work for them.

Naturally, it took me a considerable amount of time before I knew enough about China, the land, and its people to make such a suggestion. It certainly didn't happen overnight!

In fact, my first trip to China was a real eye-opener, and one I think you'll enjoy:

A Foreigner Abroad:

A Funny Thing Happened on the Way to China

1985 marked my first trek into Asia. The four-month trip took in South Korea, Taiwan, Singapore, Hong Kong, and China. As I waved goodbye to my daughters, one five- and the other eight-years-old, I was unaware of the physical and mental challenges that lay ahead of me.

Traveling to Asia sounds so exotic, glamorous, and expensive, and it is all of those things and so much, much more, but twenty years ago things were very different from the way they are today.

As a small business startup, my finances consisted of the funds I had borrowed from my Mother and Father, not to mention the three loans on our home. What I lacked in money, however, I knew I made up in unparalleled optimism and confidence. (Too bad I wasn't selling those!)

The airplane trip consisted of a deep discounted ticket, which accurately represented the seat I was granted when I boarded the plane that fateful day in the mid-80s. For those of you who've only flown business or first class to date, that's the one by the only working bathroom in economy class, which doesn't recline and is always across the aisle from the baby with the ear infection.

Thirteen hours later, I was officially starting my trek in Seoul, Korea. After two hours pushing my way through immigration, customs, and crowds of people who couldn't have cared less about my unparalleled optimism and confidence, if only I'd get out of their way, I realized that my contact, Mr. Park, was nowhere to be found.

"Okay, Irl," I thought to myself as I waged war at the taxi stand, "you are now officially an international businessman. You can handle this." Confidence never leaving me, I somehow found my way to the $8 dollar a night hotel I'd booked, sight unseen.

The surprises were far from over, starting with the room, which was approximately six feet by twelve. For those of you not privy to a slide rule at the moment, I'll translate: My college dorm room was larger.

From its window I looked directly across an alley, ten feet away, into a laundry exhaust fan which presented me with odors that faintly reminded me of home, that being my family's farm.

That night I drifted into a fitful but self-satisfied sleep that was abruptly halted by an unwelcome intrusion that would last the duration of my stay: Each day, at precisely 6 a.m., the door would burst open and there, to my amazement, was a young man with a chemical mask, a tank on his back, and a manual pump sprayer. Quickly he circled the room spraying anti-cockroach spray only to disappear as fast as he had entered.

It proved to be the most effective, if intrusive, "wake up call" I've ever had. By the time I left Seoul I had my timing down to the point where I could get up, shower, dress, and pass him by at the door. This accomplishment was always met by a smile as I passed my intruder. Maybe it was a smile of relief at not having to view me in my panic as I showered or dressed madly as he entered.

Sometimes, looking back, I think he was timing his entrance to embarrass the new guest. Then again, maybe he was just doing me a favor. Such is the beauty of China, and that elusive seventh side of the dice.

With a few phone calls to some prospective factories, my job of interviewing soon began. My first rounds of discussions were held at the hotel's small restaurant during the first week of my visit. The small tables were covered with a grey tablecloth that turned into a gleaming white one every Monday. (I am sure both came from my favorite laundry.)

A CLUE THAT I HADN'T CHOSEN A FIVE-STAR HOTEL FOR THE SITE OF MY FIRST MEETING...

I quickly discovered that the evenings were the most enjoyable time of each day. Alleyways were crowed with both merchants and customers, each vying for the other's attention and proffering or sampling an array of exotic, colorful goods. It was a veritable cabaret of sights, smells, and sounds, and I do believe such scenes were the beginning of my love affair with Asia.

Sitting with a few patrons in a sidewalk café, leaning against a vendors' cart or negotiating for a dozen mangoes gave me an insight regarding this lively people's culture, local politics, and perhaps most importantly their views of western business people.

From these alleys I gained my real, practical education. Mixing with the local people provided me with a great deal of knowledge, the kind only hinted at in the guidebooks or brochures I'd read in preparation for my trip.

It was through one of these "alley discussions," in fact, that I found that a few Japanese companies were considering pulling out of South Korea and relocating to China. This information gave me an important advantage while negotiating in the days to come. I eventually gained considerable concessions from a factory that was losing business from a Japanese company pulling out.

After five days, I had grown accustomed enough to my surroundings to the point where the number of people using the hotel surprised me. It surely was a popular one, with crowds of young girls and men of all ages in the lobby, elevators, and hallways at all hours of day or night.

By the end of the sixth day, I had interviewed over 15 different factories and was setting out to visit three of them, when in came my contact, Mr. Park. As Mr. Park was apologizing profusely for his tardiness, I could see that he was obviously nervous, looking constantly over his shoulder and moving slightly to avoid the crowds of friendly young women in the crowded hotel lobby.

This being overly apparent, I asked him if he was looking for someone. He expressed his concern, explaining quite frankly – and as it would turn out helpfully – that it was not appropriate for a "person of his position" to be seen in "this kind of a hotel."

I checked out that afternoon ...

Rule Number 1:

If the Hotel is Cheap, It's Usually for a Reason

China 101:

A Historical Perspective

China is more than just a vast and accessible land of wealth and opportunity. It is a living tapestry rich in custom, tradition, and history. In fact, some historical perspectives of the country we're talking about might be useful as a background and a reminder of this great country.

A significant aspect of China is its long cultural and national history. The Chinese people have shared a common culture longer than any other group on Earth. The Chinese writing system, for example, dates back almost 4,000 years, making it the oldest continuously used writing system in the world.

The imperial dynastic system of government, which continued for centuries, was established as early as 221 BC. Although specific dynasties were overturned, the dynastic system survived. China was even ruled at times by foreign invaders, such as the Mongols during the Yuan Dynasty, from AD 1279 to 1368, and the Manchu's during the Ch'ing Dynasty, from AD 1644 to 1911, but the foreigners were largely absorbed into the culture they governed.[2] It is as if

---

2　Caroline Liou and M.C. Alexander, China (Lonely Planet Publications) 2000

the Roman Empire had lasted from the time of the Caesars to the 20th century, and during that time had evolved a cultural system and written language still shared by all the peoples of Europe.

Throughout these many centuries, China has often been a rich and influential power on the world stage. The Tang Dynasty saw China become a sophisticated economic and military power, admired across Asia. The Song Dynasty brought about an apex in cultural and intellectual pursuits, while the Ming Dynasty witnessed widespread Chinese exploration at sea.

The dynastic system was ultimately overturned in 1911, and a weak republican form of government existed until 1949. In that year, after a long civil war, the People's Republic of China, with a Communist government, was proclaimed. This government and the ruling Communist party have controlled China ever *since.* Although the dynastic system has disappeared, the People's Republic occupies essentially the same territory and governs the same people as the Chinese Empire.

Whereas China has known periods of immense power in the past, following the emergence *of Deng Xiaoping* and his policies of economic liberalization, the culture and potential power of China seem stronger in the late 20th century than at any other period in history.

The roughly 5,000 years of history covers many dynasties … the discovery in 1963 of the earliest human in China dating back to 600,000 BC … in the time of Confucius, about 551-479 BC, a code of ethics was developed that has dominated Chinese thought and culture ever since… conflicts between nomads and settled farmers are always a continuing feature of Chinese history … and internal war after war after war, the last one being Mao's takeover in 1949.

The good news for China was the eventual rise of Deng Xiaoping. With his foresight, the People's Republic has become, both economically and politically speaking, a critically important player on the world stage today.

So now we've learned about China, but what did *I* learn?

Read on …

WHAT I LEARNED:
7 LESSONS FROM MY TRIP TO CHINA

Obviously, my eyes had been opened to new people, new cultures, a new language, new customs, and new ways of doing business. By the time I finally reached China, in fact, I had learned a few valuable lessons.

Some of them centered around *how* to do something. Just as many of them, however, taught me how NOT to do something. I share them with you now in the hopes that you can learn from my freshman mistakes and not make your own:

1. *Never Underestimate Cultural Considerations During Business Negotiations*

Just as you wouldn't tell sexist jokes in mixed company during the negotiating process in America, likewise you must learn to be what I call "culturally considerate" during international negotiations.

I didn't give you that little history lesson a few pages back just to fill blank pages; I wanted you to be aware that China's history and culture go back centuries, and can't be learned overnight. Still, I've found the Chinese to be just as willing to teach as they are to learn, and sometimes watching a Chinese negotiation in progress can be your best learning tool.

Just as in any other negotiation, watching before acting is as important as listening before speaking. It's doubly important in China, however, where customs are time-honored and breaches of protocol not so quickly forgiven.

Leeway is naturally given to their American counterparts, but be careful not to abuse the privilege by ignoring cultural considerations. Here are some of the most important, and most effective, in my opinion:

2. It's the "Little Things" That Matter

Old history is alive and well in today's Chinese businessperson. In fact, old cultural traits continue to poke their head over the shoulder of the "new" Chinese businessperson all the time.

For instance, that businessperson may wear western clothes but sport a long fingernail on his little finger. What does that mean? In old China it represents the fact that he doesn't have to work with his hands like a common laborer. In essence, it represents his "intellectual" ability.

What does a pinky finger have to do with doing business in China, you may be asking yourself. All of this has an impact on how business can (and does) get done on a daily basis. That's why I say "it's the little things that matter."

This is why a building doesn't get finished when an election is in progress, because the building (the process) wasn't as important as the "real" overall goal (the election). It can be very frustrating to those of us coming from a western perspective. The western businessman often holds the primary goal to be the "sale," whereas to the Chinese businessperson it may be only one of many goals he has on the table.

3. Time is On Their Side

If the American philosophy concerning time can be summed up in the following line from a popular Queen song, "I want it all; I want it now," then the Chinese philosophy on time can best be lifted from a Rolling Stones tune: "Time is on our side!"

A Chinese government official once told me that if, "we don't like your President's policies….we'll just wait for another four years." This is very indicative of the Chinese way of doing business. If you are a type of businessperson that cannot wait for the "walk" light to turn green…then China will be frustrating for you. The concept of time is very, very different there.

4. Remembering Self-Sufficiency

If we look at the actual characters that make up the word "China," it really means "Middle Kingdom."[3] This is a good representation of a China that never depends on "outside" support. Until the late 1800s, in fact, the outside world was not important to the Chinese.

This fact shows up in business negotiations today. The Chinese are wonderful hosts (featuring lavish dinners, drinks, etc.) but when you have desired technical support (or product) it gives them a high sense of tension (sense of distrust, being cheated, etc.).

Not surprisingly given this source of tensions, swings of highly sophisticated negotiations blended with highly immature fear and distrust can be demonstrated within moments of each other, making it necessary for you to be a patient study of character to know when something is just a knee-jerk reaction to outside influences – or a bluff.

5. Being a Team Player

Being a team player is very important to doing business with the Chinese. One thing that really sticks out is their sense of conformity, commitment, and a very strong sense of "group" togetherness. Therefore, sticking one's neck out is a very foreign gesture and is usually avoided if at all possible. However, this all encourages a sense of suspicion with people from the "outside."

This is one area where you can talk about "face" as it's basically how you are viewed by your peers, superiors, etc. (In other words, everyone!) I have literally seen sensitive test equipment stay in the box for months because the Quality Control Engineer was too embarrassed to admit he didn't know how to use it.

---

3   Caroline Liou and M.C. Alexander, China (Lonely Planet Publications) 2000

6. *It's Not What You Know …*

… but who you know…" This really gives a simple statement about the Chinese business person. They really know how to use the "who you know" way of doing business. Talk about an old boy's network. Doing business in China is a complex weaving of the "who's who" in their personal list. It's one of the mainstays within the Chinese businessman's personal armor. This way of doing business is both powerful and bulky, in that it slows down independent decision making and makes for a lot of gatekeepers to navigate and hoops to leap through once you do.

RECOMMENDED READING

There are hundreds of books about negotiating with the Chinese and even more on cultural considerations. To start your own personal library I would strongly recommend picking up a book called *The Art of War* by Sun Tzu. It's a good starting point, but there are so many different authors' interpretations that it would be impossible to list them all here. Just get one that you can read on the next plane to China….then re-read it on the way back!

PROTOCOL POINTERS: A THRU Z

(Okay, how about A Thru F?)

As we have seen, protocol is extremely important when negotiating with the Chinese. To save you from experiencing some of the hard-knocks I took to learn this stuff, here is a quick list of the best pointers I've found so far:

a. Avoid making exaggerated gestures;

b. Don't touch them;

c. No displays of public affection;

d. Use an open hand and NOT one finger to point;

e. To beckon, use palm down and wave fingers toward the body;

f. Don't put your hand to the mouth (it's considered disgusting);

[NOTE: Items a – f were taken from a book called *Kiss, Bow, or Shake Hands* by Terri Morrison, Wayne A. Conaway and George A. Borden Ph.D. I would recommend this book to the readers as a primer on protocol overviews. Best of all, it's simple, fun and easy reading. It has about 3-6 pages each for 60 different countries.]

To perhaps motivate you a little further in how important it is to take Chinese traditions and customs seriously, here are a few other things to consider: Did you know that at the present rate China's GNP will exceed the United States by 40% in the year 2020? If that's the case, then we better be effective and efficient when we are doing business across cultures.

Avoid Being Seen as "The Ugly American"

It's important to celebrate our differences. If you open yourself up to a cultural exchange of ideas, and not just focus on the bottom line of business, your travels abroad can become so much more than business trips!

This is a hard task to accomplish, however, if you insist on being what I call "overly American" at every turn. This includes being unwilling to appreciate or even recognize significant cultural fads or phenomena in your host country. For instance, what books, movies, plays, etc., are your hosts talking about at dinner? Don't ignore them because they seem too complicated; embrace them so you'll have something to add to the conversation.

Other faux pas include turning up your nose at traditional dishes, customs, or traditions; ordering American meals at every turn, bragging about how great "such and such" is "back in America," etc. You get the picture.

You certainly don't have to give up yourself to negotiate a business deal in China, but it never hurts to pay deference to a host country's rich, vibrant, and exotic culture by at least being willing to try new things.

Mentors Matter

Whether you decide to do business in China, Vietnam, Russia, or India, it behooves you to try to find a mentor in your country of choice to help bridge the inevitable cultural, societal, and political gaps that consistently arise during international business dealings.

This isn't as tricky as it sounds. In fact, I found that *finding* a mentor is very easy….finding a *good* one is a different story. The primary method is through your business contact…sorta my cousin introduced me to his old professor who introduced me to his third wife who introduced me to her old sorority sister's best friend who was the second cousin of Chairman Mao. Silly as this seems, it's one of the primary ways of finding a great mentor.

Other ways are via your US Commerce offices in the country of choice. Another good way is to check with your local World Trade Center (about 20% of them are certified to really give you superior assistance).

Remember your old college professor? He may know someone who is just right for you. As with any other business endeavor, always keep your contacts alive and well. Send them birthday cards…send them Christmas cards….use your computer to help you remember the various dates of importance and set-up virtual reminders to help you when you get busy.

Other Tips:

A mentor can be either in-person (very personal) or informal (distance communication i.e. phone, email, etc.). I have a variety of mentors that I rely on all over the world. What is a mentor, exactly? One of the most common types of mentors are those who render assistance without expectation of getting paid.[4]

Here are some other great ways to find a mentor:

- Call the chamber of commerce;

- Local organizations (Toastmasters, etc);

- Enroll in a college class;

- Search the Internet;

- Research business organizations (World Trade Centers, etc.);

- Attend conventions that would attract your type of mentor;

- Ask your present customers;

- Search out books and articles on your topic, then contact the authors;

- Read biographies of people who have been successful in your area, then call them;

- DON'T BE AFRAID OF THE PHONE – PICK IT UP!

If you'd prefer to go with someone you know and trust, or at least have formed a previous relationship with, consult local universities and their international studies departments for mentors who would be wiling to tutor you on the customs awaiting you on your trip, or who might even be willing to accompany you on the trip.

The price you'd pay for their travel expenses would be well worth their expertise.

---

4   Lowe K. Finding a Business Mentor (Entrepreneur.com) 2001

"I" is for Information

I can't stress this one enough: Read everything you can get your hands on regarding the country and its people. This is especially helpful if you can't find a mentor, as mentioned above, but even if you do I encourage you to not rely entirely on him or her.

Today is the information age, and there's never been more of it out there. Over and above maps and guidebooks, there are many valuable reference books, magazines, and even Websites devoted to China and its culture, its people, its customs, its traditions.

Do some browsing and find the book, periodical, or Website that's right for you and absorb it like a sponge. From proper protocol to common phrases to appropriate versus inappropriate gifts or gestures, you're sure to find a wealth of information waiting for you, if only you'll just take the time to look.

Ask Questions; it's Cheap

Like I said, your best asset going into any foreign business endeavor is information. If you can't find it in a book or online, or if something new or unexpected arises during your trip, never be afraid to ask questions. Far from making you look ignorant or putting you in a weak light, it shows your willingness to learn, adapt, and familiarize yourself with your new surroundings.

If you're still uncomfortable asking a business prospect, be nosy back at your hotel and ask the concierge, front desk clerk, or even other guests. The information you receive will be timely, local, and best of all, FREE!

Learn from Someone Else's Mistakes

In addition to learning from my mistakes, don't forget to learn from others as well. For instance, if a company – or several, for that matter – has failed to win the business of the company you're wooing, try to find out why.

What did they do wrong? Were the numbers off? Was it the project? Did something breakdown in the negotiations process? It never hurts to ask and the information you could receive in reply could just prove priceless when you succeed where others have failed.

Don't be Afraid to Get Your Hands Dirty

Successful businesspeople, be they on the domestic or international front, know that to truly succeed you can't be too busy, too important, or too proud to get your hands dirty. Much like a great restaurateur can't be afraid to wash a dish or clear a table now and again, neither should you be afraid of seeming common or rough by "getting your hands dirty."

International travel is fraught with miscommunication, clashing cultural considerations, and an air of surprise and unexpectedness that is rare in domestic business. Software is incompatible, outlets the wrong current, whatever the reason, things may and most likely will go wrong.

If you're afraid to do a presentation using cue cards and props or to demonstrate a product or service yourself because your interpreter or assistant failed to show, you're revealing a major weakness to your prospective international client: A lack of spontaneity.

China has survived for centuries – and is poised to become one of, if not THE major economic force in this century's economy – not because it relied solely on tradition, culture, and custom, but because it has allowed itself to change, adapt, and modify its outlook toward the future while not sacrificing any of the above.

There is a lesson to be learned here ...

FOCUSING ON CHINA

Back to our story: By now I was three months into my trek and felt quite confident in dealing with cultural differences. By this time, I was quite successful in establishing some contacts with some very competent people. In essence, I felt like I was more comfortable putting my financial eggs in this particular basket. More than anything, I felt that visiting China was a great opportunity as many of my new friends expressed their views that China was rapidly becoming the world's new "economic giant."

Since 1979, it seemed, all eyes were turning to China. By the time I entered China in 1985 there were already stories of quick successes and expensive failures. I was determined to be one of the former, and not the latter.

Prior to my arrival one of my friends introduced me to a Hong Kong resident who conducted weekly visits to China inspecting his garment factory. He invited me to join him to visit Guangzhou to enjoy an upcoming trade show. From beginning to end, the trip was a real eye opener.

It was just a few years prior, in 1979, that Deng Xiaoping decided to open up the country for free trade and marked the beginning of the most amazing economic growth the world has ever seen, in addition to the greatest reduction of poverty the world has ever seen.

I was amazed at what I witnessed firsthand during the trade show. Never before had I seen so much excitement about the future from nearly everyone I came into contact with. People from all over the world were negotiating for products that ranged from textiles to minerals; from electronics to agriculture products; from tanks to airplanes. China's economic growth was not just on the move, but was sprinting toward its own particular destiny.

During this time in China, I negotiated preliminary relationships with a number of factories. Ten years later, we still have successful business ventures with some of these same factories and, more importantly, have made very loyal friends in a country where friendship is second only to loyalty.

From my first dealings with China in 1985 until 1993 my company not only focused on China but also South Korea, Taiwan, Hong Kong, and Singapore. Such was the business climate in these regions that during that time frame I made over 25 trips to these countries and expanded my company over six times.

During 1993, in fact, I was seriously pursuing setting up our own factories in China to capitalize on this growth potential without involving so many middlemen. Thus began my odyssey throughout China. The trip began in Beijing and then branched out to cities TainJin, Xian, Shangahi, Shenzhen, and Guangzhou and finally ended in Hong Kong.

Upon my arrival in Beijing, the capital and ideological center of China, I was immediately immersed in non-stop business and cultural activities. An individual who had been assigned to us by local officials introduced us to China in a way that seemed to leap straight off the pages of the cultural and historical texts I'd been reading about the region.

In rapid succession thereafter, we accumulated knowledge about China's political, economic, and investment environments and their potential from experts, including a Vice Premier of China, representatives of the Central Bank, state ministers in charge of various sectors of the economy, and western businessmen, all of them enthusiastic about their success to date after "trying their luck" in China. We were wined and dined in a variety of settings, including the Great Hall, where 19 state ministers joined us.

In Shanghai, then and now the business center of China and the home of 14 million people as well as the Shanghai Stock Exchange, we were impressed by the dynamic "hustle and bustle" of the thriving city. After some observation, our second impression was of the tremendous *effort* being put forth to build the city into the business center of the "New China." As in Beijing, we were treated to an endless round of briefings, dinners with Chinese officials and Chinese and western businessmen, and many factory site visits.

Thankfully, not every moment of the trip was devoted to business. Shanghai is a wonderful, exciting city and I was determined to see more of it than its conference rooms and financial institutions. During those rare days when I was free from meetings, Karaoke bars, and long dinners, I enjoyed the freedom of a typical tourist.

Even when I wasn't conducting "business," per se, I still managed to learn something new about financial dealings with the Chinese. One such day I began shopping for a few silk rugs to adorn my new home. Feeling quite confident in my dealing with the Chinese to date, I began negotiating for a number of silk rugs. By the end of the day I had negotiated what I felt was a very reasonable price. Excited with my agreed upon purchase, I instructed the business establishment to carefully ship my prize to my home in the USA.

ECONOMY CLASS ASIAN STYLE

During my previous visit throughout southern China I had purchased a number of fine pieces of furniture and instructed my office to crate and ship via ocean freight. However, after carefully folding the silk rugs they required a small enough cubic space to ship via air. This I instructed the vendor to do as I departed. Fortunately, I paid by credit card as the prized silk carpets never arrived in the USA.

Lesson learned? There were a number of mistakes made during this transaction that I call "rookie mistakes." Without listing them, suffice it to say that I now use an employee to handle the logistics and shipping of my personal products. This is actually a rare occurrence in China, but like anywhere else in the world a buyer must use his diligence to ensure you receive the expected product and/or service.

If Beijing is the historical, political, and ideological center of China, and Shanghai is the developing business heart of the region, then Shenzhen is the upstart young challenger to both.

Twelve years previously, Shenzhen was a simple mud village set in rice paddies. Then it was designated a "Special Economic Zone." At the time of my visit in 1993, it was home to millions of people, large skyscrapers, thriving businesses – both domestic and foreign – and a new second stock exchange. (The population is now 6.5 million!)

Even then, it was a city to rival many found in the western world. Again, we had a full schedule of briefings, tours of industries, and endless meals with local officials and business dignitaries.

My trip ended in Hong Kong, a place where we could reflect on how such economic development could take place in just 14 or so years. Simply put, China's development started with agriculture. Then, when their people had enough to eat and most of Maslow's hierarchy of needs had been officially met, the government turned its attention to making the country attractive to foreign capital.

First to come was money from overseas Chinese. (An asset that even Russia does not have.) Then western capital started to flow. This capital initially tended to be concentrated in Hong Kong and from there it was ultimately funneled into China, where it was welcomed and immediately put to use.

By the time I finished my 1993 visit to China and Hong Kong, there was not a single soul in my company who was not impressed with the transformation that was taking place in this financially volatile region.

Almost universally, there was a belief that the future potential of China was nothing short of overwhelming. Thus the question in my mind was how to best take advantage of what I had seen and heard during my travels abroad. I was so impressed that on my return to the United States, I immediately initiated action to start the development of a new factory in China.

By 2000 my factory was not only up and running, but also having an enormous growth rate that was almost intimidating in its potential. During my visits around this time I was already hearing miraculous stories about China. These stories centered on two main issues, those being:

1. How the growth rate, if maintained, would put the Chinese economy bigger than that of Japan and the United States in the year 2020[5]

2. How the Chinese middle-class consumer population, a principal target of foreign consumer goods producers, over 100 million at the end of 2000 was heading to 500 million by 2005.[6]

Thus emboldened, I wanted to see for myself the changes that were occurring deeper in China and to determine the future business opportunities for my company. Thus I began my second major trek of China in 1997.

While not even going to Shanghai and the coastal regions, two of the fastest growing areas in China, I was nonetheless astonished at the growth of China in just four short years since I'd been there last.

A visit to the stores in central China found hundreds of local Chinese consumers spending money on rudimentary and luxury items. Although there is still a large poverty-stricken population, and although American name-brands are still hard to find, mostly because of pricing and high tariffs in some instances, both local and Hong Kong brands emulating foreign ones are snapped up

---

5   Shira D., 2004 Business Guide to Shanghai and the Yangtze River Delta (China Briefing Media, Ltd) 2003

6   Ibid

at prices which are low by U.S. standards but high as a ratio of Chinese earnings.

With great growth comes great disparity, and I would be remiss to ignore some of the obvious local issues with pollution and waste handling. During the visit in Xian, I was expecting a city of color and excitement. What I found was a city covered in coal dust giving a dull color to a once thriving, vibrant, city.

Dust shmust: Coal was towering over some smaller buildings in tall, six-story high mounds! Coal still being the primary heating source in the region, people with carts, bags, cars, or any means available were madly loading and packing this precious cargo off to their homes and businesses. (It is the hope of the government that condition will improve with the successful completion of the proposed Three Gorges Project.)

We also saw plenty of poverty along the Yangtze River, which is another reason given by the officials for the positive impact of resettlement for the Three Gorges Project. We saw crowded conditions in large cities, but despite what most westerners would consider "overcrowding" people looked content, busy, and were spending their disposable income.

Whether or not you subscribe to the same outcome as most economic forecasters, you cannot dispute the fact that the livelihood of the average person in China and the opportunities available today cannot be matched anytime in China's 5000 year history.

As far as political matters were concerned, the leaders I met were not the paranoid, autocratic, and ideological leaders often painted in the west. I saw a China very confident of its position in the world, its relations with the outside world, its economic reform, and the overall direction in which the country was headed.

From top to bottom, the Chinese believe in what they are doing and they are dedicated to continuing China's economic development. Being nationalists, they know this is the only way to get more respect in a post-Cold War world dominated by the United States.

CHINA'S CURRENT ECONOMIC & POLITICAL REALITY:

Fact vs. Fiction

It is important for you as a potential international businessperson to understand that only a few years ago there was a sweeping leadership transition in China, during which the youngest and best educated group since the founding of the PRC was installed!

It started at the Communist Party's 16th National Congress in November, 2002, when Jiang Zemin handed over his "CEO" post to Hu Jintao, who was actually selected in the early 90's for that job by Deng Xiaoping. In March 2003, at the 10th National People's Congress (their version of parliament), the Premier Zhu Ronji passed his job to Wen Jiabao.

The most positive, unexpected, and additional changes were in the Politburo, the party's top decision-making body, when over 60% of the members retired in favor of a younger set! At the March 2003 gathering, in fact, all eight vice-premiers and 18 of 28 ministers were new ... and there was comparable turnover among the party secretaries and governors of the 31 provinces.[7] The bulk of these new leaders grew after Deng Xiaoping opened up China to globalization in 1979, the reason why I could establish businesses relationships in 1985 in the first place.

It is a legacy sure to influence China's bright future.

But a development not without its fair share of risks ...

SOME OF CHINA'S CHALLENGES

If we listen exclusively to the economic forecasters, life over the next few decades sounds like little more than a bed of roses for

---

7   Shira D., 2004 Business Guide to Shanghai and the Yangtze River Delta (China Briefing Media, Ltd) 2003

China. But let's take a quick look at some of the amazing challenges
China is facing (Note: some of these observations also come from
Lyman Miller, editor of *Hoover's Chinese Leadership Monitor*).

Change is never easy, and today China is learning that fact firsthand. Three decades of reform to shift to a market-driven economy tied into the world economy has caused hundreds of millions
of dislocations, deep social tensions for tens of millions of Chinese,
as well as great economic opportunities and wealth for tens of millions of others.

A widening of the gap between the "haves" and the "have-nots,"
surging unemployment as millions transfer from the country to the
cities, uneven economic development between coastal and interior
provinces, enormous official corruption, the media still centrally
controlled, and outdated public services present problems of gov-
ernance on an unimaginable scale. Finally, the Chinese banking
system is a mess and could be the cause of an economic meltdown.

But just how fragile is the Chinese banking sector?

In a recent study, Charles Wolf of the RAND Corporation
pointed to the inherent fragility of the financial system in China.
According to Wolf, the balance sheets of China's four major state
banks are riddled with non-performing loans. Estimates of their
total value vary, but they may amount to more than 60% of China's
GDP, or $1.6 trillion. [8]

Should China experience a run on its banks, large-scale capital
flight, a significant reduction in savings, or a decline in capital for-
mation, the ensuing financial crisis and credit squeeze could lower
annual GDP growth significantly and have an enormous impact on
the region and the global economy.

On the subject of foreign policy, one of China's biggest questions remains how to deal with the U.S. They need our trade, but
not our overwhelming power. They will continue to advance national unification of Taiwan, a situation with some risk. Most experts agree that China needs to continue globalization and deal
with the negative economic and social consequences such engagement is creating.

---

8   Russell G., China (WTCT, Tacoma, Washington) 2003

THE DRIVE TO VIETNAM

During China's development of Shenzhen it was becoming apparent that there were a few shortcomings. Traffic has always been an insane mix of confusion, impatience, and apparent lack of any and all rules whatsoever. The road system throughout China is marginal in some areas, and nonexistent in others. This was really apparent during an adventure several colleagues and I had during a recent road trip!

One weekend my staff and I were discussing the various vacation points in China. One of my staff pointed out that a small town near the border of Vietnam was a very desirable location, with clean beaches and a warm pleasant climate. With no apparent means to get there other than bus, we confidently decided to drive.

Having decided early in my career that Chinese traffic was not a place for a cautious American, at the time my company had two cars (each with a very competent driver). So we loaded up the SUV and headed out for what we thought was a 4 to 5 hour drive. This drive turned into about 12—13 hours but along the way it opened our eyes to the country, in general, and to the overland transportation system, in particular.

The roads were a mix of dirt, gravel, and pavement, by that I mean to say occasionally there was one of the above, sometimes two, and more often than not a mix of all three! About halfway to Vietnam we bounced upon a very wide, four-lane highway that would rival any modern freeway system in the US. To our concern, the beautiful road disappeared from under us as quickly as it appeared as we bounced down a steep incline to, again, a dirt road. This amazing, surprising, and beautiful road was a 10-mile jewel in the middle of dirt roads leading to it and away.

Again and again, the road wound its way through village after village. Unknown to us, our driver diverted our trek to his village. Presenting me with his village's temple and a consultation with the local fortuneteller brought me to a deeper understanding of how rural China functions. What I thought was the same language could not be understood due to the dialect. I noticed that even though two people were speaking Mandarin they might not be able to understand each other, as the dialect is so strong in each particular province.

By the time we arrived at the border, we were exhausted. For our troubles, the only signs we saw were those posted by the town warning us not to use the beaches due to the pollution. As we stood staring out onto the blackened beaches, the rain began with a vengeance.

The trip was highlighted by playing Maja throughout the night with the local people, drinking soju, and discussing American television with the locals. The whole while the village's young children were fascinated with these white-skinned western people in a small village in an area of China where hardly anyone visits or, for that matter, hardly anyone ever leaves.

Rule #2:

It's always greener on the other side of the fence ...

JOB LOSS FROM THE U.S. TO CHINA:

Menace or Myth?

Economic forecasts aside, you might be hesitant to do business with China due to the political climate in our own country. As for negative feelings in the United States, all you hear today from the political left in this country is about "job loss to China." The fact is that a recent study of global manufacturing by Alliance Capital Management showed that manufacturing jobs are declining across the globe, from the U.S. to Europe to Japan to Brazil, due mainly to the growing automation and technology raising the productivity of manufacturing globally.

From 1995-2002, 22 million manufacturing jobs were lost globally. You might be surprised to learn that, despite the hype, the U.S. wasn't even the biggest loser: we lost 11% of our manufacturing jobs during the period, Japan lost 16%, Brazil lost 20%, and even China lost 15% due to huge losses among old state enterprises. Manufacturing is going the same way as agriculture did, historically speaking. In 1910 one-third of American workers worked in agriculture, today less than 3% do, but production has risen dramatically.[9]

Myth buster: *From 1995-2002, while manufacturing jobs globally dropped by 22%, global manufacturing output rose by 30%. Overall, U.S. manufacturing job loss has very little to do with trade or low wages in poor countries.*

Weighing in on the matter, the CEO of 3M says, "We don't manufacture in China to eliminate U.S. jobs, we do it to be competitive."

What's happening is more related to productivity than trade or "exporting jobs." As Tor Dahl, America's reigning expert on productivity, explains:

> *In a recent study that will be published in June, we were able to pinpoint the main reason for the jobless recovery in the U.S.*
>
> *It followed from the dramatic cost cutting of U.S. companies during, and following, the 8-month recession of 2001. One company's cost is another company's revenue. The cost cutting companies had, on the average, lower productivity improvement than the U.S. business sector, and lower profits and growth as well. From 1998 through 2002, employment in those companies decreased by about 2%, while the U.S. labor force expanded by 1.2%.*
>
> *The most productive companies, however, had higher profits, higher growth, and they increased employment by 34% over the same 5-year period!*
>
> *The myth that productivity destroys jobs is effectively demolished by this study. It is lack of productivity that destroys jobs ...*

---

9   Russell G., China (WTCT, Tacoma, Washington) 2003

When one looks beyond the alarmist headlines and political rhetoric, the logic behind making China and India popular scapegoats for the loss of American manufacturing and service jobs simply does not hold up. U.S. manufacturing employment peaked in 1979. The most recent above average drop in manufacturing jobs reflects our amazing increase in productivity, our economic down side from 2000 through 2002, and the decline in exports due to the prolonged world economic recession. But unlike Japan, China and India are allowing American companies to participate in its growth. General Motors, for example, faces a simple imperative: invest in Asia to take advantage of the region's cheap labor and its fast growing economy or lose out to rivals from Europe, Japan, and elsewhere.

Recent facts from China offer some perspective on this challenging and controversial matter: Shun Chui's transformation from no paved roads and no motor vehicles to an industrial town since 1987 is typical in China. Multiply that by the 700,000 villages of China and you begin to appreciate the implications of China's industrial revolution. One study found that China accounted for 25% of the world's economic growth from 1995 to 2002 (measured by purchasing power parity). More than the U.S.! We ought to keep in mind that China *does* possess 20% of the world's population!

China has become a major consumer of U.S. manufactured exports, such as electrical machinery and numerous types of components, among other goods. China is a major importer of agricultural products from the United States, and U.S. service providers have been increasing their share of China's market in many sectors as well. It is also interesting to note that China's imports are growing faster than its exports, up 40% in 2003.

China is our third largest trading partner and although imports from China are more than our exports to China, exports are growing much faster than imports. Specifically, in the last three years, our exports overall are - 9%, but exports to China are +62%! Some 50% of China's exports come from foreign-owned factories of the multi-national corporations. Of China's 40 top exporters,

10 are U.S. companies. China exports $12 billion annually to Wal-Mart, accounting for 10% of all Chinese exports![10]

To remind us of relative size factors, China's strength is manufacturing and in the U.S., manufacturing is only 14% of our output with 11% of our jobs. India, on the other hand, is focused on services, which is 60% of our output involving 66% of our jobs. And for the consumer, a big part of our economy, China drove down the costs in manufacturing, such as Wal-Mart in retail and India in services.

So let us remember that doing business with China is not all bad for our consumers!

THE NEW LEADERSHIP *IS* ADDRESSING SOME OF THESE CHALLENGES

The new leadership in China is beginning to show that they are not ducking these, and other, issues facing their own country and ours. Specifically speaking on some of the country's biggest issues:

- SARS...they finally created transparency!

- The Iraq war ... they were opposed at first but, when it happened, they quieted down ... they need oil big time in the years ahead and some will come from Iraq, particularly if Iraq is free!

  China will exceed all importers of oil possibly as early as 2020 and needs to find that oil with a totally different approach. As an example, on January 31st China's oil boss signed a deal to buy crude oil from Gabon, Africa. President Hu Jintao arrived the next day to celebrate this new Sino-African cooperation. No proclamations of third world solidarity, no lambasting of American imperialism, certainly no lauding of democracy. Just business "with no political conditions," as President Hu put it to Gabon's parliament.

10   Russell G., China (WTCT, Tacoma, Washington) 2003

Africa has oil and China has bottomless demand. A perfect match!

- China is lending a critical helping hand to diplomatically solve the North Korean nuclear proliferation risk.

- China has now been a member of the WTO for more than two years, having acceded to the WTO on December 11, 2001, after 15 years of negotiations with the United States and other WTO members. Under the terms of its accession, China committed to a set of sweeping reforms: implementation of the WTO's market access, national treatment and transparency standards; protection and enforcement of intellectual property rights; disciplines on the use of trade-distorting subsidies; and other changes to bring its legal and regulatory system in line with those of other WTO members. China viewed joining the WTO as a means to preserve and expand China's access to export markets abroad, particularly the United States. In turn, other WTO members envisioned that faithful WTO implementation by China would reduce the ability of the government to intervene in the market to direct or restrain trade flows.[11]

China has made important headway since its WTO accession two years ago, and has completed much of the nuts and bolts work of WTO implementation. It has reviewed thousands of laws and regulations and made changes necessary to effect many of its WTO commitments; established new transparency procedures in many national and sub-national ministries and agencies; and reduced tariffs to their committed levels, among other things.

Despite these gains, China's compliance with its WTO commitments has, over the past two years, been uneven.

The U.S. administration is determined to continue to address market access problems that contribute to our trade deficit with China and to ensure that China operates with fair, transparent, and predictable rules. That means,

---

11   Russell G., China (WTCT, Tacoma, Washington) 2003

most importantly, that China must live up to the commitments that it made upon joining the WTO. We also need to ensure that China engages in fair trade when it comes to its exports to the United States. Our companies want, and are entitled to, a level playing field.

Steps such as emphasis on collective leaderships, transparency from leaderships meetings, commitment to public welfare, and holding leaders accountable show a steady shift from the old communist system to a much broader open system. It sounds to me like the Russian "managed democracy!"

FOREIGN DIRECT INVESTORS:

Their Views

Foreign Direct Investors "walk the talk." ... those numbers are now higher than FDI to the U.S.! And a personal observation from our team in Hong Kong managing the Asian Infrastructure Fund that will surprise you:

A comparison of doing business with Chinese partners vs. U.S. companies: As long as you select well in China, there is a real spirit of honoring the terms of the deal, even though those terms are much less extensively documented than in the West.

There may be a number of after-investment negotiations to resolve issues, but in our experience it has always been done within the framework of the spirit of the deal. With American companies, the deal is extensively documented with countless pages of legalize. But after-investment issues have sometimes resulted in the spirit of the deal going out the window, with lawyers trying to find loopholes in the literal wording of the agreements. This difference in business culture probably would surprise many Western investors, who often imagine the worst in dealing with local Chinese partners. We pick

*our Chinese partners well, and we have a solid and well-connected
Chinese staff to help us with that. We have certainly all heard less
than flattering stories about the behavior of local partners.*

*A second point of interest: despite the U.S.'s free market image,
it isn't the leader in private transportation infrastructure development. Australia is, and that is why we sourced so much investment from Australia. Privatized toll roads, ports, and airports are
the norm in Australia. They are almost non-existent in the U.S. -
Europe, depending on the country, is somewhere in between.*[12]

WHAT DOESN'T WORK

A few years ago I was talking to a staff member belonging to the
Ministry of Health in Beijing. He was working on a plan to fund
hospitals needing equipment during the upcoming year. Knowing
that there has been some mystery regarding how these departments
fund projects I asked him about the methods of determining the
cost associated to purchase and supply the project.

He responded with a shrug and a despondent answer: "I just get
whatever money they give me and I buy what I think is necessary."

"No statistical data?" I replied.

"I am sure someone is conducting the process," he shrugged.

Now, let's fast forward a few months. I was talking to an
International Marketing Manager of a medical firm. The young
man was experienced with the European markets and was recently
very successful competing throughout the EU. He decided not to
enter into the Chinese markets as his data analysis showed that
the disposable income per capita is not enough to warrant their
efforts into China.

Fast forward *another* six months: Their major competitor, a
European factory, concluded an 86 million dollar contact with the
Ministry of Health. Even though the European factory was 12%
higher in cost.

---

12   Russell G., China (WTCT, Tacoma, Washington) 2003

Rule Number 3:

Always remember who is spending the dollar ...

CHINA'S FUTURE [13]

Are You in it?

Viewed over the very long run, Asia has had only a couple of bad centuries and the real changes for China have been going on since 1979 when Deng Xiaoping adopted globalization. Their subsequent return to the center of the world economy is a natural outcome, given the size of their population, their high level of education, and their entrepreneurial skills and ambitions. As a matter of expectation, China is very likely to pass the U.S. economically – and militarily – in the first half of this century!

Regardless of how fast China grows, our country's sheer power, experience, alliances, geopolitical position, and influence will continue to convey upon our leaders tremendous responsibility. (I hope they understand that!)

The question is: Will China continue to open up, become more "pluralist," and move toward becoming a democratic nation joining the global institutions in a responsible, constructive, non-confrontational way? Or will it seek to perpetuate the Communist Party's monopoly power, limit free speech, and become more con-frontational and obstructionist challenging the global economic and political institutions to best suit Chinese interests?

Of course, China is not alone; we have similar questions in our own country. As the most powerful country in the history of the world now, will we use that power constructively to continue to

---

13   Ibid

lead on issues of peace and trade, seek to build consensus and collaborative solutions with allies in Asia and Europe to the world's political, security, economic, and social problems?

After all, that's how we built the post war global political and economic order that has delivered unprecedented prosperity across the globe. Or will we retreat from the difficult, sometimes frustrating challenge of consensus-building and continuing to build on existing global political and economic institutions, and fall back to more of a unilateralist and isolationist foreign policy out of frustration and a more protectionist trade and investment policy out of fear from growing competition from China, Asia, and elsewhere?

Listen for yourself: The noise level in the U.S. is loud against globalization. It doesn't matter that from the early 1980s through much of the 1990s we experienced an incredible period of American prosperity. This was a time of great expansion of America's integration into the world economy, with Clinton totally behind globalization (something he still is today)! Yet, following our recession, if you watch much of the debate in this political season, or tune into Lou Dobbs at CNN, you'll be told that free trade is a "mortal threat to America." The arguments are contemporary versions of those used in the 1930s...or in the 1980s with regard to Japan. Much of the brouhaha boils down to one simple question: "How can we compete with hordes of cheap labor overseas?"

Unfortunately, the question is much broader in scope and focus than that and our people don't seem to understand the connection between their prosperity and what's happening in the world economy.

While the speed of capital and technology transfer has increased dramatically, and the world is highly competitive, who's to say these are bad things? Frankly, I think they're good! All participants in the global economy can benefit. Hundreds of millions of people in the world have been lifted out of poverty in just the past two decades. No matter what the spreadsheets say, how can that be a *bad* thing?

Our response as a country should not be to complain, but to significantly improve our lagging educational system so our workers' skill-set can be aimed at where our shortages exist. Microsoft, for example, can't fill the new jobs they need with Americans because of our outdated system of education!

In my view, the Chinese government understands that the shift to globalization and free market behavior has been the cause of China's rebound and they cannot, and will not, stop that force. Maintaining their communist central "dictatorship" will not work in the long-term the more open China becomes. It was a reality, however, to read in the *International Herald Tribune* on February 14, 2004 the following paragraph:

> *There may be few communists left in China, but the spirit of Lenin is alive in Beijing. Hong Kong is learning that the secretive, centralized party in Beijing has yet to yield to the forces of the marketplace...*

However, they will one day, and I hope it is a *peaceful* yield!

FURTHER OPTIONS AND OPPORTUNITIES IN CHINA – EVALUATING FOREIGN-OWNED ENTERPRISES 3

You may be wondering why China rates two chapters in this book as opposed to, say, Vietnam, for which I only wrote one. Well, considering the fact that most forecasters predict China will be the #1 economic giant during the next few decades, I felt this goldmine of opportunity rated twice the amount of pages as the rest of the countries we'll be discussing.

Frankly, as well, China is a land of contrasts. Verdant fields and erupting cherry blossoms war with drab concrete cities of hulking skyscrapers and jarring neon signs touting everything from Coca-Cola to Nikon.

Here, too, the Chinese prefer to keep their personal and professional lives separate. Like us, the Chinese work hard and play hard, yet not necessarily at the same time. Though Chinese business lunches take hours, they are far from the three-martini lunches of American lore. They might call it lunch, but trust me: It's work!

So whereas my first chapter on the startling, stunning, surprising, and scintillating world of China was in large part anecdotal, in this chapter I wanted to get more specific. You might want to consider Chapter 1 a Chinese business lunch, and Chapter 2 a business dinner. Thus the purpose of this chapter is to provide businesses with new options to carry out expansion in China.

Here I have provided basic information on the relevant taxation and other related regulations governing the Wholly Foreign-Owned Enterprises (referred hereafter as WFOEs) investment and operation. In addition, I compare the Manufacturing WFOE with the Trading WFOE, along with its locations in and outside the Free Trade Zone within China.

My company currently holds a representative office in Shenzhen, which does not allow us to conduct trading business in our own name, and a holding company in Hong Kong, which *does* allow various activities.

My parent company, A/D Electronics, is located in the Pacific Northwest. As business grew, I began searching for an alternative business vehicle that would provide my organization with more opportunities and protection. My recent selling of a manufacturing facility inside of China provided challenging lessons that prompted my exploration of the WFOE, and in so doing I learned a wealth of information that I would like to share with you now.

Due to my investigations, I intend to set up a WFOE in the Guangdong province of China held by a company incorporated in Hong Kong (or the United States) named A/D Electronics.

Once established, our particular WFOE will be engaged in importing electronic products and medical equipment from all over the world. Our goal is to sell to domestic markets as well as international markets. As a WFOE we will conduct simple packing, assembling, client fulfillment, and provide warehousing, much as I suspect many of you might were you to be in the same situation. These functions will be in addition to our manufacturing business.

I admit the process was intimidating at first, but once all the pros and cons were weighed and the benefits proven to outpace the drawbacks, it was soon clear that the process was well worth the headaches. I share this information with you in an effort to show you both sides of the coin, and in as clear language as possible, the contents of this chapter summarize my investigation into WFOE's.

Regulations Governing WFOE's

Much as the name implies, Wholly Foreign-Owned Enterprises, or WFOE's, refer to an enterprise established within the Chinese territory in accordance with the relevant Chinese laws and with all the capital being invested by a foreign company, enterprise, or other economic organization or individual.

In order to establish a WFOE, the foreign investors must make a significant investment in cash or equipment and registered capital must be commensurate with the size of the operation and the social and economic liability of the enterprise. The profit obtained and other lawful interests of a WFOE are protected by Chinese laws.

WFOEs are owned exclusively by one or more foreign investors (either corporate or individuals) and can therefore offer a mechanism for better control over management, technology, know-how and operations. To make matters even simpler for the entrepreneur, there is no need to have a Chinese partner to form a WFOE.

Still, you *are* dealing with a foreign country and no matter how eager China is for your business, it is up to you to do your due diligence in the forming of your WFOE and, to that end there are some definitions to wrap our heads around.

The Examination and Approval Procedures of WFOE:

Legal Status & Limited Liability Definition

WFOE's are limited liability companies with the status of a Chinese legal company. This means that the shares are 100%

held by foreign individuals and/or companies. The term "Limited Liability" is recognized by the amount of registered capital injected into the business. Although this may in fact be a combination of two assets, cash injection *and* equipment, the total value of these also represents the extent of the WFOE's liability. Under these quite normal circumstances, it is important to understand that in the event of a bankruptcy the parent would be expected to make up, via injection, the difference between the required registered capital amount and the actual paid in capital.

Registered Capital Requirements

These vary from industry to industry and to make matters more confusing also vary on a regional basis. It therefore makes sense, if location of the WFOE can be flexible, to shop around and compare regional capital requirement differences. Like any big move, and don't think for a minute that opening up an international entity isn't a big move, research and investigation is key to achieving ultimate success.

Wherever you site your WFOE, however, basic investment criteria remain the same. As an example, the minimum registered capital in selected areas near Shenzhen is HKD 1,000,000, or USD 130,000, which must be paid in one lump sum within six months.

The WFOE must have a registered capital in relation to its total investment. The capitalization of the WFOE is the total amount of capital contributed by the investor and registered with the authorities, i.e. the "registered capital."

The required ratios between registered capital and total investment are presented as follows:

Total Investment	Percentage of Registered Capital to be injected
Less than USD 3 Million	70% or more
USD 3 to 10 Million	50% or more
USD 10 to 30 Million	40% or more
More than USD 30 Million	33 % or more

Capital contributions may be in the form of land use rights, cash, machinery and equipment. As a caveat, please be aware that the final valuation of these is done by the Chinese Commodity and Inspection Bureau, so your control over this aspect may be limited. Other capital contributions may include intangible property such as industrial or intellectual property rights, which can be valuated up to a maximum of 20% of the registered capital.

The Foreign Investment Bureau will look at the general viability of the project and the reasonable cash requirement for a particular type of investment. The Company Law and the Accounting Regulations do not mention any specific ratio requirement for registered capital contribution, although a maximum may be 70% as new plant and machinery and 30% in cash. Be aware, however, that this is not written in stone and the cash investment requirement may be higher. The Bureau will require a numeric percentage expressed in the Feasibility Report and WFOE's Articles of Association for issuing the approval certificate.

At least 15% of the registered capital must be paid in within 90 days of obtaining the business license with the rest of the contribution to be completed in between 1 to 3 years, depending on the registered capital.[14]

---

14   Shira D., 2004 Business Guide to Shanghai and the Yangtze River Delta (China Briefing Media, Ltd) 2003

The various deadlines versus contributions are as follows:

Total Registered Capital (in USD)	Final date of contribution to reg. capital
500,000 or less	Within one year of licensing
500,000 to 1,000,000	Within one and a half year of licensing
1,000,000 to 3,000,000	Within two years after licensing
3,000,000 and 10,000,000	Within three years after licensing
More than 10,000,000	Time limit to be examined and approved by the examination and approval authority in accordance with the actual circumstances

CHOOSING THE RIGHT LOCATION

For most businesses, identifying the right area for factory/business is certainly one of the biggest issues to contend with, and it's no less, if not more, of an issue when vying for space overseas.

Sometimes, the decision-maker rushes into a lease or purchases contracts on the basis of initial gut feelings or recommendations rather than on the basis of a detailed evaluation. I can't caution against this rash course of action enough and in so doing offer the following two words of caution: Never assume.

The process of doing a detailed evaluation of any prospective area for your factory or business may be time-consuming and complicated, but the price for ignoring this crucial step could be costly, if not prohibitive, in the long run. As is the case with any new endeavor, the early bird doesn't always get the worm, but occasionally even gets the shaft.

In China, the landlord is not allowed to lease the property if he/she does not possess a property right certificate. Sometimes a substantially lower price is offered for this reason, so beware such easy come-ons. Before choosing a final site, you need to check if the landlord is the legitimate owner of the property and possesses relevant permits. A lease contract normally needs to be recorded at the property administration bureau.

ENVIRONMENTAL ISSUES

China, in general, and Guangdong province, in particular, are becoming more and more aware of their environmental problems and are taking stricter measures to protect their natural resources. If the production of your WFOE involves pollution, be it substantial or minimal, it is likely that you are not going to be allowed to set up in areas close to water reservoirs or other protected areas.

I have personally seen several companies lease premises and begin setting up facilities only to find out later that the environment bureau required them to move to another site. One can imagine the amount of capital, not to mention time, which often means the same thing, lost in such a costly oversight.

Even though it is possible to push the application through and stay in the chosen location (by successfully going through all necessary assessments and pollution disposal and protection procedures instructed by the environmental bureau) things would have been a lot easier if this environmental assessment was done in advance.

Again, when doing business overseas one can never do enough due diligence ...

General Establishment Procedure

There is simply no way around the bureaucracy: Different authorities *will* be involved at different steps of the approval procedure for any foreign entity in China. Being forewarned will hopefully spare you the aggravation of surprise, as throughout the incorporation process you will become more and more familiar with departments like the Administration of Industry and Commerce, the Bureau of Foreign Trade and Economic Cooperation, the state and local tax bureaus, the Customs and so forth.

The Ministry of Commerce is the final approval authority for a WFOE. However, this final authority delegates part of its power to its local counterparts, the Bureau of Foreign Trade and Economic Cooperation at provincial or municipality levels

For your convenience, here are the examination and approval procedures for the establishment of WFOE's:

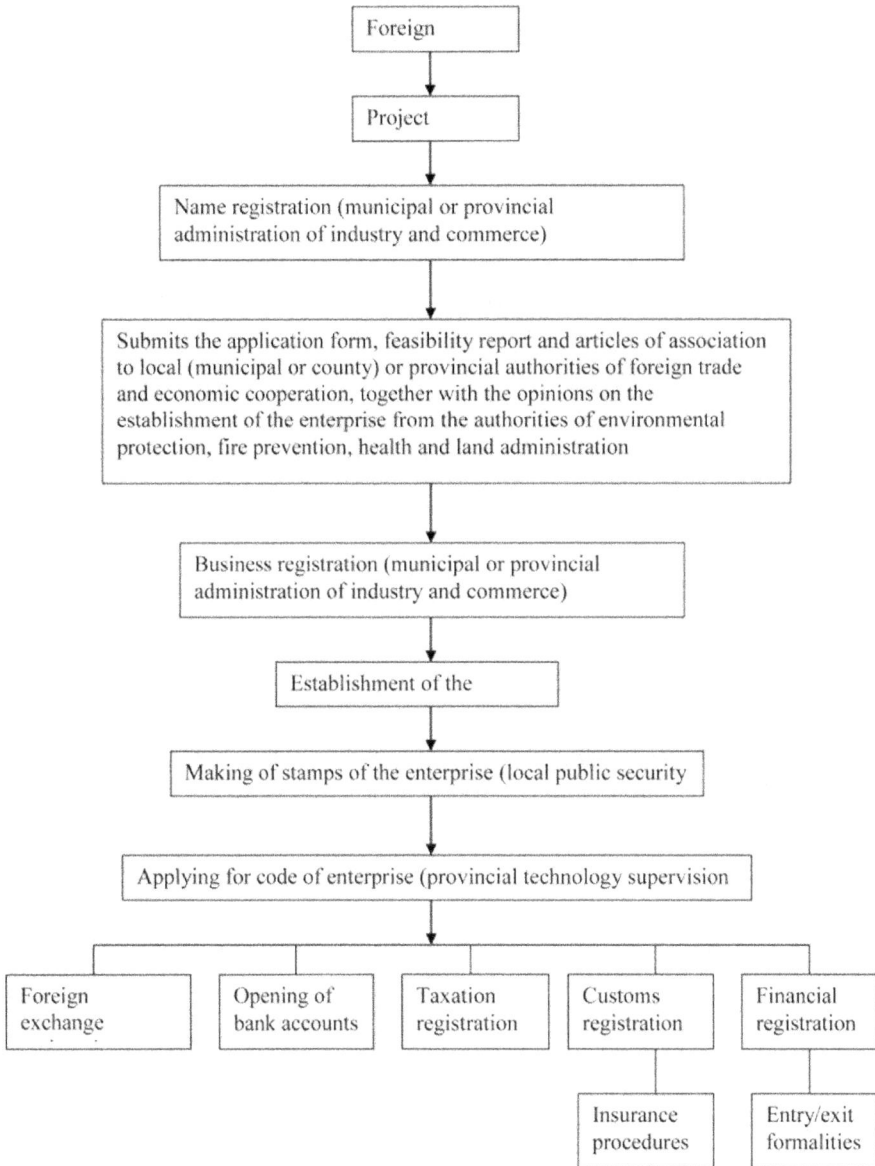

```
                    ┌──────────────────┐
                    │    Foreign       │
                    └──────────────────┘
                             │
                             ▼
                    ┌──────────────────┐
                    │    Project       │
                    └──────────────────┘
                             │
                             ▼
         ┌────────────────────────────────────────────┐
         │ Name registration (municipal or provincial  │
         │ administration of industry and commerce)     │
         └────────────────────────────────────────────┘
                             │
                             ▼
 ┌────────────────────────────────────────────────────────────────┐
 │ Submits the application form, feasibility report and articles    │
 │ of association to local (municipal or county) or provincial      │
 │ authorities of foreign trade and economic cooperation, together  │
 │ with the opinions on the establishment of the enterprise from    │
 │ the authorities of environmental protection, fire prevention,    │
 │ health and land administration                                    │
 └────────────────────────────────────────────────────────────────┘
                             │
                             ▼
         ┌────────────────────────────────────────────┐
         │ Business registration (municipal or          │
         │ provincial administration of industry and    │
         │ commerce)                                     │
         └────────────────────────────────────────────┘
                             │
                             ▼
              ┌────────────────────────────┐
              │ Establishment of the       │
              └────────────────────────────┘
                             │
                             ▼
     ┌────────────────────────────────────────────────┐
     │ Making of stamps of the enterprise (local       │
     │ public security                                  │
     └────────────────────────────────────────────────┘
                             │
                             ▼
 ┌────────────────────────────────────────────────────────┐
 │ Applying for code of enterprise (provincial technology   │
 │ supervision                                              │
 └────────────────────────────────────────────────────────┘
                             │
```

Foreign exchange	Opening of bank accounts	Taxation registration	Customs registration	Financial registration
			Insurance procedures	Entry/exit formalities

OPERATIONS:

Management Control

Whatever your current chain of command, China recognizes a specific business paradigm for its WFOE's. In this case, the board of directors is the highest level of authority and decides the main policies of the WFOE as well as making the key decisions for its business development.

To handle various operational issues, the board of directors also appoints a general manager. The GM is responsible for managing the daily operations of the WFOE. The chairman of the board is, by definition, the legal representative of the company. The board shall consist of at least three directors, or be a single executive director.

You may choose to set up an appropriate sized board, so that it can fully reflect the foreign investor's intentions and purposes, but flexible enough to operate the WFOE. The general manager of the WFOE is responsible for the daily operation and executes the resolutions and decisions of the board by which he/she is appointed or removed.

Legal Status

As with any company, legal issues are of tantamount importance in this day and age of a litigious society, be it domestic or international. As an individual entity, the WFOE has the status of a Chinese legal person with the right to use properties, carry out management and production independently and sue and be sued. The liability of shareholders is limited to the WFOE's registered capital.

Land and Buildings

Remember, Dorothy, you're not in Kansas anymore. Accordingly, all land in China is owned by the state or by local collectives. The rights to use the land may be granted to the WFOE or holding company for fixed periods of time, the normal period being 50 years for commercial use. Land users may assign, mortgage or lease to a third party land use rights that have been obtained through payment of a land-grant fee.

Value Added Issues

The Customs Office will check the selling price of final goods in order to make sure at least 25% profit is raised from the manufacturing, processing and assembly procedure. This is not written in stone, but should be completed with in practice. Therefore, simple assembly operation may not be approved if your intention is to set up a manufacturing WFOE.

Profit Repatriation

A WFOE must maintain its accounting books in China and have them independently audited every year. Profits may only be distributed after full payment of income tax and the making up of any previous year's losses. Foreign investors have the right to remit profits abroad after the WFOE has made the required allocations to its reserves/bonuses/funds. In addition, it can also deduct losses from previous years.

Foreign Exchange Restrictions in the China

There is a strong control over foreign exchange in the Peoples Republic of China, or PRC. All foreign exchange income should be remitted back to the home country of the investor unless re-invested into China operations.

The foreign currency to be used by the WFOE as expenditures can be withdrawn at local banks by producing the "Certificate of Foreign Exchange Registration" that has passed annual inspection and other relevant documents. Likewise, remittance of dividends and stock bonuses require documentation and agreement from the board of directors and proof of tax payments.

WFOE's can open foreign currency and RMB accounts in China. There are three types of foreign currency accounts that can be opened in the PRC by a WFOE:

> **Capital account** used to receive the registered capital invested. The foreign currency is deposited here and can be exchanged into RMB.

> **Trade account** used to receive or remit the foreign currency related to the business operations. In this account the WFOE can keep only a limited amount of foreign currency and the rest must be exchanged into RMB.

> **Foreign Loan account** used to receive or repay a loan from a holding company or other parties. The amount of money deposited in this account can be kept as foreign currency or exchanged into RMB.

Transfer Pricing

The profits after tax gained by foreign investors in the WFOE can be remitted out of China. However, if the sales of final goods are made to associated companies or the holding company and not to the final client directly, there may be a transfer pricing issue to consider.

The selling price to the end users should be the same for sales to associated enterprises as well as for sales to independent and unrelated third parties. If the selling price from the WFOE is deemed to be too low (according to market price) by the Tax Bureau, it may be possible that the price would be arbitrarily adjusted by using the following methods of calculation:

> the comparable uncontrolled price method;

> the resale price method;

> the cost-plus method;

Remember: The business must be aware of this when making its calculations so that undue losses are not incurred.

MAIN TAXATION ISSUES FOR WFOE

Value Added Tax

The Chinese government stipulates that all units and individuals engaged in the sales of goods, provision of processing, repairs and replacement services, and importation of goods within the territory of the People's Republic of China shall pay a Value Added Tax, or VAT.

The VAT rate is generally 17%, and for some goods at 13%. For small-scale taxpayers it is 6%. The VAT tax payable shall be the balance of output tax for the period after deducting the input tax for the period. The formula for computing the tax payable is as follows:

Tax payable = Output tax payable for the period –
Input tax for the period

The domestic sales fundamentally changes the tax situation of the WFOE as it is subject to import duties (variable dependent upon product, location and final customer in the production/sales circle) on any non-China sourced components and VAT (17%) on sales.

For example, the "exempt, set-off and refund" method applies to my particular case. "Exempt" means that no VAT is levied on export sales, "set-off" means that the WFOE can set-off the local purchase VAT input against the local sales VAT output, "refund" means that the WFOE can get a refund of the local raw materials purchases VAT-input used for export sales.

If the WFOE does have domestic sales, then it should charge output VAT on local sales. However, if the VAT paid on inputs is bigger than the VAT charged on domestic sales, then such an additional amount can be refunded.

Enterprise Income Tax

The general rate of taxation in the PRC is 30% payable to State bureau and 3% payable to local tax bureau, with total at 33%. Tax holidays are applicable to my company and enterprise accordingly:

> ➢ "…two years of corporate tax exemption and three years of 50% reduction" from the first accounting profit-generating year for **manufacturing enterprises** with an operation term of more than 10 years.

> ➢ The general corporate income tax rate is reduced to 15% in the Special Economic Zones of Shenzhen, Zhuhai, Shantou, Xiamen and Hainan Island.

> ➢ The general corporate income tax rate is reduced to 15% in other special areas in the country like Economic and Economic and Technology Development Zones.

> ➢ The general corporate income tax rate is reduced to 24% in Coastal Open Areas like the Dong Guan area. Plus 3% of local tax, total 27%.[15]

---

15   Shira D., 2004 Business Guide to Shanghai and the Yangtze River Delta (China Briefing Media, Ltd) 2003

Withholding Tax

To ensure your low tax exposure, a neat method is to charge your own WFOE services from your parent. These can include: royalties for trademarks, patents, licensing fees, professional memberships, management expertise, group sales and marketing costs, group research & development costs, etc.

These services can be billed to your WFOE as legitimate expenses, for example on a quarterly basis. Withholding Tax applies to the invoice for the service (this is currently lower than China's Income Tax so it saves you money).

On the other hand, a foreign company without a permanent establishment in the PRC is subject to 10% withholding tax. This tax is based on all income from China including interests, rents and royalties. However, note that the profits gained by a WFOE in the PRC are exempted from withholding tax.

Individual Income Tax

Individual income tax in China is levied on wages, salaries and other income of foreign nationals and local residents. As far as foreigners are concerned, the amount to be paid depends on the position of the individual within the WFOE, the length of their residence in China and the source of their income.

Monthly income from wages and salaries is taxed according to a progressive scale rate, ranging from 5% to 45 %. The first 4,000 RMB of the foreign individual earnings in China are tax-free. [16]

For your convenience, the total IIT liability for foreign staff can be calculated as follows:

---

16   Shira D., 2004 Business Guide to Shanghai and the Yangtze River Delta (China Briefing Media, Ltd) 2003

Salary after tax free threshold reduction	Tax Rate	Quick Calculation Deduction
To RMB 500	5%	RMB 0
RMB 501-2,000	10%	RMB 25
RMB 2,001-5,000	15%	RMB 125
RMB 5,001-20,000	20%	RMB 375
RMB 20,001-40,000	25%	RMB 1,375
RMB 40,001-60,000	30%	RMB 3,375
RMB 60,001-80,000	35%	RMB 6,375
RMB 80,001-100,000	40%	RMB 10,375
In excess of RMB 100,001	45%	RMB 15,375

As far as any local Chinese staff you may employ is concerned, IIT is applicable as well as the welfare fund which could be as high as 45% including pension fund, social and medical insurance, unemployment insurance and housing funds. Naturally, the business must be aware of this ratio for budgeting purposes.

Custom Duty

Custom duty should be paid on imported equipment. This duty is based on the equipment value determined by customs if the WFOE license mentions "local sales." Custom duty should be paid for imported raw materials if the final products are sold domestically.

On the other hand, custom duty does not apply if all the final products are exported.

Comparison between Manufacturing and Trading WFOE

Manufacturing WFOE's have been allowed to sell up to 50% of their production onto the domestic market. At the end of 2004 restrictions on internal versus export sales requirements were lifted. This change will make it possible for WFOE's to sell the majority, if not all of their production, in China. This will allow businesses to participate into the increasingly attractive local market. For those wondering whether or not the time is right to move to China, this is one more critical point to consider.

For some time it has been difficult to establish WFOE's in service (trading) industries in China. WFOE's have been restricted to "manufacturing, processing and assembly" operation. However, some local governments turn a blind eye to bending these rules as long as the trading WFOE's was sited in a Free Trade Zone. Fortunately, it is now permissible to set up pure trading WFOE's and buy and sell on the domestic market. A comparison of both services is as follows:

Comparison between Manufacturing and Trading WFOE

ITEM	Manufacturing WFOE	Trading WFOE
Minimal Reg. Capital	HKD 1,000,000 (USD130,000)	At least USD 300,000 (varying with different FTZs)
Location	No restriction	Now only available in Free Trade Zone
Area of premise	At least 400 square meters	80-90 square meters in practice generally

Value Added Tax	Entitled to "exemption, set-off and refund "	"levy in advance and then claim back." For local purchase: pay the VAT at first and get refund after export sales For export sales: VAT output free If in Free Trade Zone, no VAT duty
Income Tax	Enjoy "two years of corporate tax exemption and three years of 50% reduction"	No tax holiday

Comparison between WFOE in and Outside Trade Free Zones

It is common for WFOE's, especially if they are involved in manufacturing or an added value process, to be sited in what are known in China as "Free Trade Zones," or FTZ's. Not surprisingly, these FTZ's are commonly situated next to ports with full import / export facilities, customs and bonded warehouses. Despite the corruption that still plagues China today, there *are* a variety of honest companies that can assist in logistics, warehousing and transportation.

    Free Trade Zones are useful because they allow the importation of product into the zone Import Duty and VAT free – and they remain that way until either exported (no charge) or enter the domestic market proper – at which point the VAT (usually 17%)

and pertinent Duty kicks in. So what's in it for you? Basically, that means you can manufacture, process, assemble and even store product in the zone free of duties until either re-exported or sold.

Businesses must evaluate their market mix (domestic versus foreign sales) in order to determine if locating within a FTZ is beneficial. To help assist you, I have provided the following chart listing the various policies and procedures involved:

COMPARISON OF POLICIES BETWEEN A FOREIGN COMPANY SET UP INSIDE AND OUTSIDE A FTZ

Item	FTZ	Non-FTZ
Registration of enterprises	Both Manufacturing WFOE and Trading WFOE are permitted	Trading WFOE are allowed only after 14 December 2004
Taxation		
1. Value Added Tax for inventory	Enjoy " Exemption, Set-off and Refund "	Same as FTZ
2. Custom Duty for imported Raw Materials	Exemption – Imported RM used to exported finished goods Levy – Imported RM used to local sales	Same as FTZ

3. VAT and Custom Duty for self-used equipment	Total exemption	1. Exemption for encouraged enterprises 2. Levy in advance and refund later for 100% export-oriented enterprises 3. VAT and CD levied – Other enterprises
4. Enterprises Income Tax	1. 15% 2. Enjoy " two years exemption and three years half rate starting from profit year "	Same as FTZ
5.Custom Administration of imported Raw Materials	Tax deposit isn't needed	To be paid in the first year based on the VAT and CD of imported Raw Material. If the enterprises are graded to "A category" in the second year, tax deposit isn't needed.

Foreign Exchange Administration

1. Verification and Cancellation Formalities	No needed	Needed All the receivable collection of exported goods must be received within a defined period of time
2. Settlement	Either foreign currency or RMB	Only RMB The circulation of foreign currency is prohibited

Operation

1. Exhibition	No deposit is required for the imported exhibited goods and no time limit	Licenses required Deposit required for imported exhibited goods Time limit for returning the goods
2. Bonded warehouse	No compulsory regulation on time limit	The time of goods stored in the warehouse is limited to 1 year
3. Rental	Factory: HK$30-45 Office: HK$55-60	General: RMB11-15

TO WFOE OR NOT WFOE:

Important Considerations and Conclusions

When it comes to the final question, "To WFOE or Not WFOE," time may just be on your side: The "Foreign Trade Law of the People's Republic of China" amended on April 6, 2004 by the Eighth Commission of the Tenth National People's Congress took effect on the 1st of July 2004. The amendments were aimed to implement China's WTO commitments in relation to foreign trade.

In this amended version, "Foreign Trade Operators" as defined in Article 8 have been expanded to "individuals and legally incorporated enterprises in China," whereas in the old law, individuals were excluded. "Foreign Trade" as defined in Article 2 means "the import and export of goods and technology, and international trade in services," by which international provision of services is also governed.

It may not sound like much initially, but I can tell you this represents a *big* step forward by the government in terms of opening up to smaller international investors. Excellent opportunities are offered to the prudent business leader if they can do their due diligence to research all the factors and become a WFOE.

In summary, foreign companies will be allowed to establish Trading WFOE's starting from 11th of December 2004; all geographical restrictions for retailing enterprises will be removed.

The new regulations apply for the following activities:

- **Retailing** – i.e. selling goods and related services to individual persons from a fixed location, as wells as through TV, telephone, mail order, internet and vending machines;

- **Wholesaling** – i.e. selling goods and related services to companies and customers from the industry, trade or other organizations;

- **Representative transactions on the basis of provisions (agents, broker, auctioning);**

- **Franchising;**

- **Import/export, distribution and retailing by existing manufacturing companies;**

Limitations will still apply to some specific products such as books, periodicals, newspapers, automobiles, medicine, salt, agricultural chemicals such as pesticides, crude oil and petroleum and other sensitive products, which may or may not affect your decision to become a WFOE.

Furthermore, the new requirements set forth by the regulations substantially lower the registered capital required to set up operations in the country. Foreign investors will enjoy national treatment in setting up trading companies with minimum registered capital in accordance with the Company Law of China which means for wholesaling enterprises U$D 60,000 and for retailing enterprises U$D 36,000. If you'll recall the figures from earlier in this chapter, that requires less than half of the initial investment for the former and nearly a third for the latter.

However, a word of caution: many questions still exist on the implementation and interpretation of this new regulation so you will need to keep abreast of the Chinese trades to make sure you are aware of the latest regulations and/or fallout.

As with any move, domestic or foreign, doing business with China, let alone in China, carries with it a fair share of risk. On the other hand, I hope I've shared with you some of the many, many benefits that exist in this country ripe for growth, opportunity, and success. The choice is yours.

So is the potential for profit ...

Table 1:

Structure of Manufacturing WFOE

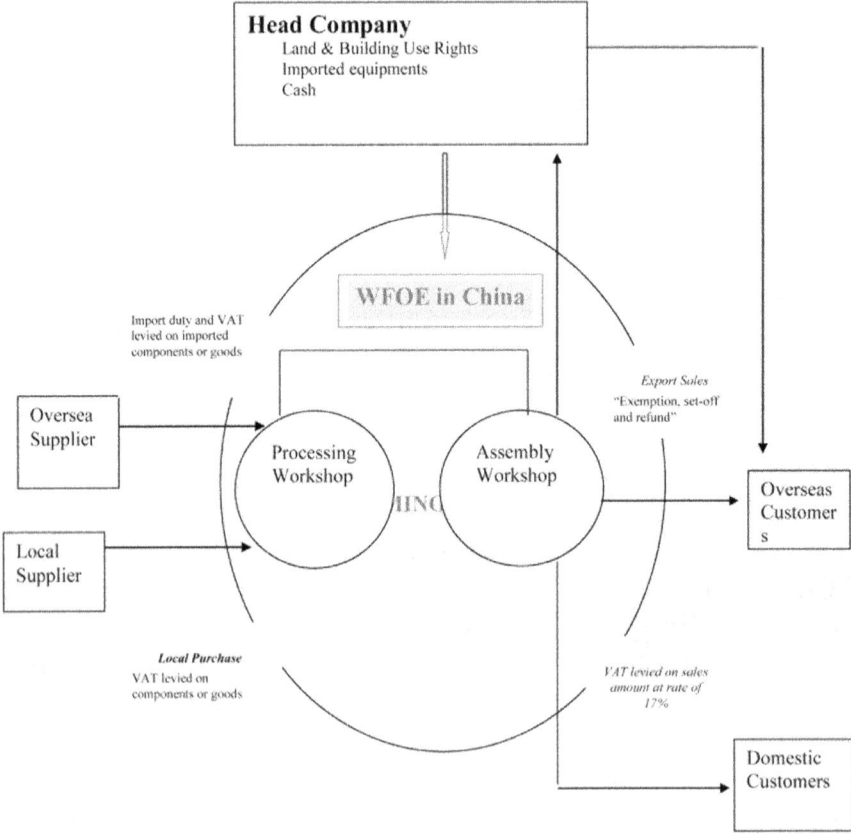

Head Company
Land & Building Use Rights
Imported equipments
Cash

WFOE in China

Import duty and VAT
levied on imported
components or goods

Oversea
Supplier

Local
Supplier

Processing
Workshop

Assembly
Workshop

Export Sales
"Exemption, set-off
and refund"

Overseas
Customers

Local Purchase
VAT levied on
components or goods

VAT levied on sales
amount at rate of
17%

Domestic
Customers

VIETNAM – SHATTERING THE HOLLYWOOD MYTH 4

"Good Morning, *Vietnam*!" It's the oft-quoted line of a favorite Robin Williams film of the same name but the modern version might be, "Good Morning, *America*! Wake up and smell the opportunity!"

At least for the entrepreneurs like you and I …

For if all you know of Vietnam comes from Hollywood, I can tell you you're missing the bigger picture of a land filled with marvelous people, beautiful landscapes, an amazing cultural background, a nearly staggering resilience, workers of creativity and stamina, and million-dollar opportunities.

Described as the next "Asian Tiger" to enter the world of trade, just after China, of course, the diverse and dynamic country of Vietnam represents a potentially huge opportunity for the manufacturer, importer, exporter, investor, and, most of all, *The Entrepreneur.*

What makes Vietnam so attractive in the first place? And why *now*? Well, naturally there are a variety of reasons that have taken years in the making to finally come to fruition, but two bullet points instantly leap to mind: The money and the people. Manufacturing costs are low in comparison with other developed Asian countries, and the work force is intelligent, educated, and hard working.

Above all else, Vietnam is a country in transition. Never before has Vietnam been so amenable to foreign business opportunities, particularly with its former political adversary, America. (A bit more on that later in this chapter.) This makes it a great time for you to think about doing business in Vietnam, and to help you do that I'd like to discuss several of the biggest factors you'll need to know to do just that.

THE BUSINESS VIEWPOINT

When did Vietnam become such a hotbed of business opportunity? Clearly, this country with its rich history and vast natural resources has always been a fertile source of possibility, but as we really start looking at Vietnam from a business perspective we see that the economy of Vietnam has continued to transition over the last ten years since the United States lifted its trade embargo in March of 1993.

A dozen years hardly seems time to become an international heavyweight, and we'll discuss some of the challenges Vietnam faces in becoming just that, but this amazing country has taken full advantage of twelve short years to create a business climate ripe with opportunity.

Although much has been made of these changes in Vietnam's economy by both those in the business community who are in favor of a capitalist and/or those arguing for a more socialist system, the transition is not nearly as fast or as far reaching as the two factions might claim.

Despite these different approaches, certain economic trends are unmistakable and bear careful note as we look to the future and prospects for further change in the economy of Vietnam.

The top three approaches, in my opinion, are:

1. Despite the increasing visibility of small shops, private restaurants, new factories, and Foreign Direct Investment

(FDI), the State Sector and State Owned Enterprises (SOE) have continued to be the biggest sector of the economy.

2. A major point to note is that the collective economy is still a major factor in overall economic activity in the economy.

3. The individual, small-owner, and private economy have continued to grow and mature, particularly in two hotbeds of modern commerce, Ho Chi Minh City and Hanoi.

Forget what you know about rice paddies and Hollywood. The Vietnam of 2005 and beyond is destined to be an economy with a strong state sector and with a growing private and individual sector that has become increasingly significant in the retail sector and is even growing in the services sector.

Collective associations, particularly in forestry, agriculture, and aquaculture remain a relatively large portion of national Gross Domestic Product, or GDP. If you're wondering whether or not Vietnam is just a flash-in-the pan, forget it: All of these changes will continue in the years ahead as Vietnam's economy continues to redefine and adjust to more and more market-based structures.

In a move to further entice foreigners to bring their money to Vietnam and invest in factories, Vietnam recently loosened central control of approval of investment licenses. What this groundbreaking step means at the ground level for you and your employees is that now new factories need not solely pass through the Ministry of Planning and Industry (MPI) in Hanoi but investors may go directly to the local level and file the forms to start a business and invest there.

As anyone who's ever done business in a foreign country can tell you, the less red tape and bureaucratic meddling at the top, the better. Skipping this step altogether means more control for you and more profit at the local level, something that immediately puts you and those you'll actually be doing business with on an even playing field.

This fact was very apparent during a discussion with a few local level government officials on one of my recent trips there. Unlike in Vietnam's quite recent past, today government processes are shortened and streamlined.

What took a few months only years ago now takes only a few days. I can't tell you how vital that is to making a realistic go of it in Vietnam, and other countries where the state is as powerful, and present, as is Vietnam's. This broad stroke demonstrates Hanoi's commitment to entice foreigners and their long-range commitment to wooing international commerce.

But it doesn't stop there: Additionally, the central government is talking about further reforms such as possibly opening up the stock market to 100 percent foreign owned companies, further freeing up the hiring of engineering and senior managers, and possibly even giving foreign firms the right to mortgage their assets.

The Ministry knows that competition for foreign investment is intense throughout the region and has even discussed possibly lowering land rental fees for foreign companies. This may not sound like much on the surface, but it's vital if outside companies are ever going to compete with locally-owned businesses: Currently land rental fees for local investors are 40 percent less than those for foreigners!

The above developments mean good news for investors. Although many of the changes under discussion are still a ways off, the change to allow investors to bypass the Ministry of Planning and Industry and go directly to the local level removes one layer of bureaucracy, resulting in a layer of chance for the diversion of funds and the once upon a time inevitable delay in getting a project started.

Even with these changes, however, much remains to be done and action not words will be what investors will be judging Vietnam on in the long run. To paraphrase Lenin, "foreign investors will be voting with their feet" to either pass Vietnam by or to stop and invest.

That is, *if* the investment climate is right.

As in China, Vietnam recognizes three types of typical business organization for a foreign company. These are the representative office, the joint venture, or the one hundred percent (100%)

foreign owned enterprise. [17]All of these have various pros and cons, but allow me to share some personal experience in guiding you toward the most appropriate category for you.

In China, a similarly state-strong country with various levels of bureaucracy, our company has had experience with all three forms. Based on this experience, we feel that as in China the time of representative offices is long past.

I also recommend staying away from joint ventures, as we believe the lack of control, problems with the law protecting minority equity participants, weak rule of law, and the lingering specter of corruption generally make a joint venture not worth the future potential problems it poses.

I therefore recommend the one hundred per cent (100%) foreign owned enterprise, which can be formed relatively quickly in Vietnam simply by applying for an investment license.

Such an application requires the following:

- A filled-out application form for the investment license;

- The charter of the enterprise;

- The statements certifying the legal status and financial capacity of the foreign investor;

- The economic-technical explanatory statement (a business plan);

- Other files stipulated in the law;

The duration of a one hundred per cent foreign owned enterprise can be up to 50 years and this duration must be set out in the charter. For those wishing to lock in a more permanent foothold the government can grant extensions to this period, but at this point these cannot exceed 70 years.[18]

---

17   Shira D., 2004 Business Guide to Shanghai and the Yangtze River Delta (China Briefing Media, Ltd) 2003

18   Shira D., 2004 Business Guide to Shanghai and the Yangtze River Delta (China Briefing Media, Ltd) 2003

Setting this aside for the moment, one still must be careful to avoid corruption and avoid internal conflict between the north (Hanoi) and the south (Ho Chi Minh City). The casual observer can easily see that the vibrant and visible Ho Chi Minh City is becoming a very progressive city.

However, Hanoi, the country's capital, has been noticeably slower to progress. This, I believe, is due to the present government and its members. Be aware that despite the recent advances made since 1993, capitalism is still looked upon with caution by the majority of those in power in Vietnam.

As a western businessperson, one must not get overconfident when working, or trying to work, within foreign countries. Unless we are very conscious of the country's culture and its history, surprises can await around the next corner.

And not all of them are pleasant.

Before I share a few of my personal experiences in this vital and vibrant land, however, I will as always share some background information to better prepare you for doing business with the Vietnamese.

PEOPLE, PLACES, AND THINGS

According to the March 2002 issue of *Corporation Relocation News*, there are about 75 million people in Vietnam today with a labor force of about 40 million workers, with an additional 1.5 million workers joining the labor pool each year.

Eighty percent of these are ethnic Vietnamese, while the remaining twenty percent comprises more than fifty separate ethnic groups. About seven million of these ethnic minorities are members of the hill tribes or mountain people, making their homes and livelihoods in the spectacular mountains of the north and central highlands. Among the many languages spoken in Vietnam are Vietnamese, Chinese, English, French, and even Russian.

As with many foreign countries, the disparity between Western/European standards of living and the modern Vietnamese earning potential is truly staggering: The minimum wage for workers is $35 per month.[19] To earn that, workers work eight hours a day, six days a week.

As witnessed at the various companies I visited personally, compared to workers in other parts of southeastern Asia, Vietnamese workers tend to be more creative in the workplace. Most of the Vietnamese workers are not made up of migrants so they tend not to move around as much, reducing turnover. The general workforce is large, inexpensive, and very well educated. Vietnam has a 95% literacy rate, which is relatively high compared to its neighboring countries.

Shaped like an elongated S, Vietnam stretches the length of Indochina's peninsula and covers a surface area of 128,000 square miles – making it roughly the size of Italy or, in the United States, New Mexico. China lies to the north, Laos and Cambodia to the west, and the South China Sea to the east.[20]

Few countries boast a more beautiful setting in which to do business. Topographically, Vietnam is a verdant tapestry of soaring mountains, fertile deltas, primeval forests inhabited by exotic fauna, sinuous rivers, mysterious caves, otherworldly rock formations, and heavenly waterfalls and beaches. Beyond nature, the curious and open-minded visitor will find a feast of culture and history in Vietnam.

For convenience, the country can be thought of as comprising three unique areas: north, central, and south. The north is known for its alpine peaks, the Red River Delta, the plains of Cao Bang and Vinh Yen, enchanting Halong Bay, and historic Hanoi as well as for the diversity of its ethno linguistic minorities.

Vietnam's climate is as complex as its topography. Although the country lies entirely within the tropics, its diverse range of latitude, altitude, and weather patterns produces enormous climatic variation. North Vietnam, like China, has two basic seasons: a cold,

---

19   United States Central Intelligent Agency, The World Fact Book (U.S. Government) 2004

20   United States Central Intelligent Agency, The World Fact Book (U.S. Government) 2004

humid winter from November to April, and a warm, wet summer for the remainder of the year.

Summer temperatures average around 70 degrees Fahrenheit (about 22 C), with the occasional catastrophic typhoon thrown in to keep things exciting. The northern provinces of Central Vietnam share the climate of the North, while the southern provinces share the tropical weather of the South.

HAZARDS IN CROSSING A ROAD

South Vietnam is generally warm, the hottest months being March through May, when temperatures rise into the mid-90's (low-30's C). This is also the dry season in the south, followed by the April-October monsoon season.

All of this is just to reiterate the fact that the many Vietnamese businesspeople you are about to meet, through my words and, hopefully, through your own personal experiences as you yourself begin to explore business dealings here, are shaped by a pulsating and violent landscape that is as unforgiving as it is unmistakable.

So are the various foreigners who do business there ...

CASE IN POINT:

The Japanese Businessman

During one of my recent visits, I had the pleasure of visiting a Japanese facility in Southern Vietnam. My young assistant (who was Vietnamese and educated in America) and I were listening intently to the Japanese General Manager as he enthusiastically gave the reasons why his employer moved to Vietnam. His passion was evident as he listed his various reasons, many of which were similar to those I've already shared with you.

During the hour, the General Manager kept referring to what he called his "Co-Creative Employees." When we asked the manager to explain this term, which was new to both my young assistant and I, he showed evidence that the Vietnamese workers increased productivity by making what he called "creative suggestions."

Continuing, this enthusiastic Japanese manager explained that factories in China required extensive documentation to ensure the worker consistently accomplished the task. Once trained, however, the Chinese worker will achieve high repeatability in their work. The Vietnamese worker can achieve the same repeatability but in addition can provide creative suggestions to improve the production and products.

Further into the discussion the General Manager shared with us his company's most impressive statistics on turnover: Amazingly, they experienced less than 3% in Vietnam while their Chinese plant was in the excess of 30%.

The Japanese manager continued his enthusiastic presentation. A highly motivated individual, he explained his passion for the Vietnamese and further captivated us in his story of developing the "co-creative" worker.

After giving our thanks and gratitude to the manger, we left the facility with a different perspective on the general semi-skilled worker in Vietnam. As we drove away, my assistant turned and said to me: "I want to work for that person...."

Without irony I replied "…me too."

Silently, I quickly began to evaluate my own company and how I might achieve the same enthusiastic response about my own employees.

Lesson #1:

Co-Creative workers soon become Pro-Active, which in turn leads to higher profits.

A WEEKEND IN VIETNAM:

Coffee, Catfish & Convenience

Throughout this book you will be reading about incidents that happen outside the workplace. I include them not for vanity's sake, or comic relief, though I must admit most of them poke fun at yours truly and his inexperience in foreign countries, but instead to show you that as much can be learned about a country *after* normal work hours as can be discovered on the job.

The following anecdote is one such occasion:

I was very excited one weekend during my travels to possibly visit an island off the coast of Vietnam. Exploring a possible paradise is personally intriguing to me and Vietnam, a land of vast beauty and breathtaking natural landscapes, held no exception. Unfortunately, all the flights out of Ho Chi Minh City were booked (seems as though many people had also "discovered" this island).

The results of this discovery found my young assistant and I discussing various alternatives to our weekend outing. Our driver suggested driving out of the city and exploring the countryside instead. Offering no other alternatives, and eager for a break from our appointed duties, we set off with no apparent destination.

Our drive was pleasant and well rewarded by frequent stops that provided much historical and cultural insight. I always enjoy discussions with the local people and am especially intrigued by the local farmers, who toil every day under much physical duress and financial burden. This gave way to a short stop by a rice field, which offered a small shaded area for the traveler to stop and enjoy a cool drink.

The predominant farming system in Vietnam is rice-based agriculture. Vietnam offers genetic diversity in the main ecosystems of the country, even though Vietnam is primarily a rice-consuming country. Case in point: Coffee.[21]

Much like tea in China, coffee is very popular in Vietnam and everyone seems to consume large amounts throughout the day. The village of Khe Sanh, a former battleground in the hills of central Vietnam, is something of an oddity: a booming coffee town amid a global coffee slump.

During the mid-1990s, when coffee prices soared around the globe, Vietnamese farmers planted coffee bushes with abandon. In a decade, the country grew from the world's 16th-largest exporter to the second, helping to create a worldwide coffee glut in the process

As we finished our drink that day I noticed a small home behind the benches. The front patio area was covered in raw rice drying in the open air. As we strolled nearby we asked permission to wander through the open rice field behind the house.

Warmly welcomed by the children and their father we carefully navigated the strewn boxes, farm implements, and various discarded items toward the open field in the distance. Nearby a small pond with fat and happy catfish literally came alive as we neared the water, as eager and open mouths scrambled for purchase while flapping flippers negotiated along our path. Never before had I seen fish so happy to see human beings.

---

21 United States Central Intelligent Agency, The World Fact Book (U.S. Government) 2004

Noticing a small bridge OF suspended planks hovering over the pond, I inquired the purpose. "Is this a fishing plank?" I queried, scratching my head. "Those cat fish are quite active."

"Ah," my assistant giggled knowingly, "the cat fish are anticipating your arrival – and use."

Confused, I waited for an explanation but did not continue my inquiry when the answer literally hit me on the nose: I noticed a strong septic odor as the wind shifted over the pond toward our direction, suddenly realizing the restroom was alive and kicking.

Lesson #2:

Never assume western conveniences will be available in a foreign land.

THE TUNNELS:

Lessons Learned; Wisdom Gained

As we continued our travels on our Vietnamese road trip the driver stopped at a nearby park along the way. It became apparent from the entrance that the park was not only large but could accommodate large groups of visiting tourists. Passing a new temple that stood testament to the park's popularity – and profit – we at last came upon the designated parking area.

I must pause here for a moment to reflect on my personal history: I never had the privilege of serving in the United States military. The height of the war in Vietnam found me silently studying at college and far removed from the politics of the day. As time inexorably passed, the war in Vietnam quickly became a distant memory. Never directly faced with war, I was thus decidedly ill-equipped for the experience we were about to encounter.

After parking the car our driver quietly informed us his desire to stay with the car while we traversed the park. If that wasn't fair warning enough, I soon learned from my young but now sober assistant that what we faced was the legendary Cuchi Tunnel Museum.

This area, I was eventually informed, is close to the area known as the "Iron Triangle," where the famed American B-52's dropped endless bombs, the entire area was napalmed and bulldozed, and the Viet Cong still lived underground in over 250 miles of intricate, claustrophobic, and hidden tunnel systems.

The park's tunnels, I was told somewhat wryly, had been greatly "enlarged," and I use the term loosely, for the typical western tourist's size as they were having trouble getting people to go in before.

As I stepped through the entrance we were informed that we could not turn back once we had committed to the tour, but must stay on the path and follow our assigned guide. I was a little suspicious when my assistant was charged about 25 cents for entrance while I was charged about $1.50, but much like I'd ignored the driver sitting this one out, shrugged it off to happenstance.

The suspicious nature was further aroused, however, when our guide appeared in a military VC uniform. (Apparently, he was a "method actor" and would choose to stay in character throughout our tour.) Young, in shape, and full of confidence he immediately began directing our march toward a nearby pavilion.

Seated were about 20 spectators intently listening as the speaker gave an enthusiastic presentation while referencing to a nearby map illustration a highly complex system of tunnels. Seeing my arrival, the narration changed to the showing of a black and white video.

Immediately, my uneasiness began to elevate: The video was a 1967-69 version of the Tunnels and the apparent "victory" against the Americans.

While disturbing, at least to me, the video was highly interesting, depicting as it did the rich and storied history of the land on which I now stood. During the Vietnam – America war there was a large presence of VC in the villages around Cu Chi. In an attempt to avoid the American Army they dug out of harm's way and created the Cu Chi tunnels.

By 1965 250km of tunnels crisscrossed the Cu Chi area. Tunnels were as small as 80cm high and 80cm wide, and some were as many as 4 levels deep and included toilets, wells, meeting rooms and dormitories as well as basic hospitals. The intricacy and sophistication of the tunnels was function over form: At times it was necessary to stay below ground for weeks on end.

The Americans used defoliant sprays and bulldozers to remove cover and sent troops down the tunnels to face booby traps, snakes and bombs, all to no avail. Finally they carpet-bombed the area.

At the time, B-52 Bomb craters still littered the park.

Once the video was over, our guide herded us toward the first tunnel. Without ceremony, in we went. My head hit the top and scrubbed off a bat, which flew on ahead. My shoulders both touched the sides, and in some spots I was on my hands and knees. (Epcot it wasn't!) Meanwhile the guide, it seemed, was sprinting on ahead with no problem.

My mind flashed back to the video I'd just seen: The thought of trying to carry munitions, cannons, running through here with saturation bombing going on above all day only to go in the rice fields at night made me weak. Ever since that day I have tried to imagine the feeling of being in that area in wartime. I now have a little better idea, but still cannot imagine the sheer terror those men must have experienced in the heat of battle.

The entrance was well-hidden, and with good reason: I later learned that they hid the entrance quickly for every new tourist group. They had a flat hatch that flipped up, reinforced with concrete, so visitors could tell a difference when pounding around, trying to find it. A little dirt was kicked over it, and the entrance was suddenly invisible. Our guide asked if anyone wanted to go in. This was not the tourist tunnel, it seemed, but a regular one.

Not surprisingly, nobody volunteered.

There were three levels in the tunnel we explored, which we were told was indicative of many, with cooking, schools, medical rooms, storage. The medical unit was a bed with a canopy, a small doctor's bag, and a light. No one knew the entire cave layout for fear of torture victims talking.

Why this story? And why in a chapter about doing business in Vietnam? By now the implication should be clear: It is important to remember this war, especially for the Foreign businessperson wishing to conduct business in Vietnam.

To this day Vietnam considers itself the victor of that historic and bloody conflict and for years afterward slowly dug itself out of the economic depression by sheer force of will.

When discussing business in Northern Vietnam with government officials, I still sense the struggle between state run businesses and private ownership. Ho Chi Minh City is dramatically changing toward private enterprise while the North still stresses over older ideals.

Alas, despite how far it's come, Vietnam is still a land of conflict …

Lesson #3:

Know where you are going before getting in the car.

CUSTOMS AND CULTURE

Anyone going to Vietnam would be wise to bone up on some of the unique customs and superstitions of the country, lest they cause confusion, misunderstandings, hard-feelings, or even loss of friendship. (Not to mention business!)

The old saying, "when in Rome, do as the Romans do" cannot be applied to the letter in Vietnam, but it is still very important that we respect certain customs and superstitions of the people who must live and work there.

Having had extensive contact with Westerners by now, many Vietnamese have begun to understand their ways and have even adopted some of them for their own use. However, there are thousands of ordinary folk whose customs have not changed in generations.

And are not likely to anytime soon ...

Customs *are* changing, but slowly. Case in point: Most of the Vietnamese in urban areas no longer bow when they meet each other. In formal gatherings, at religious places, and sometimes in the country areas, one may see the people clasp their hands together in a prayer-like gesture and bow slightly. This is not practiced to any extent in everyday life in Vietnam as it is in neighboring Thailand.

The custom of handshaking, formerly considered barbaric to the mainstream Vietnamese, is now achieving popularity due mainly to the Western influence in the country. Today Vietnamese men will generally shake hands and say the equivalent of "how are you" and tip their hats when greeting people. Women, especially those in the countryside, still shy away from shaking hands, especially with men from their own country. For that reason, it is best not to offer to shake hands with a woman unless she offers her hand first.

This is a good practice to get into anyway, be it regarding shaking hands, dining in a local restaurant, or any of a thousand little daily customs that might blip under your radar. Where as Americans tend to rush on instinct, when in a foreign land hang back a bit and watch first, then do. Listen first, then talk. You might just discover a unique custom or habit that helps you blend with the locals.

Case in point: Whereas Americans often immediately introduce themselves in given situations, the ordinary people of Vietnam think this to be rather bold and like to have a mutual acquaintance make the introduction. They will rarely introduce themselves when going into a home or office until asked to do so. This may be due to their innate shyness and modesty, or perhaps custom, but in either case it is something to be understood and, more importantly, respected.

It's All in the Name

Names carry great importance in Vietnam. Often Vietnamese will have secret names, known only to themselves and their parents. If it is given away, the person believes he is exposed to evil spirits. Except in rare cases, family names are seldom used outside of the family circle. Children are often called names in rank of birth, such as Chi-hai, Chi-ba (daughter two, daughter three, etc.).

So how do you get around this name superstition? One should call Vietnamese people by Mr., Mrs., or Miss until specifically asked to go on a first name basis. Be patient: The Vietnamese do not do this as quickly as Americans in their relationships with people.

Another thing to remember that is especially important, when in the company of a third person, your friend must be called by his name with a Mr., Miss, or Mrs. preceding it, as the case may be. If this is not done, it may suggest great intimacy or friendliness, or can also be misinterpreted as being arrogant treatment of the individual by a superior. Either one would be a check in the negative column, as seen by your Vietnamese counterpart.

Most Vietnamese names consist of a family name, middle name, and a personal or given name. The order is reverse to the American custom. For instance, the name John Paul Jones name in Vietnamese style would be Jones Paul John. However, we do not call someone by his family name in Vietnam. If we use the names Miss Hau Dinh Cam, for instance: Hau is the family name. We would call her "Miss Cam." Falling back on our earlier example, Jones Paul John would be "Mr. John." On very informal occasions, we might at their request call them "Cam" or "John," but would always add a Miss or Mr. to the name in the presence of other people outside of the group.

An exception to this rule dates back to traditional customs of long ago when beloved leaders were called by their family names. Oftentimes during the course of business one runs into locals of varying degrees of authority, education, or position. In these specific cases, it is desirable to call Vietnamese professional and government officials by their title, i.e., Mr. Assemblyman, Mr. Doctor, Mr. Lieutenant, etc.[22]

When speaking to the Vietnamese it is best to call to people in a quiet voice, using their names preceded by Mr. Mrs., or Miss. Warning: Waving or beckoning with an upturned finger is considered highly impolite by the Vietnamese.

If you must silently signal for someone to come toward you, do so by using the whole hand with the palm turned down. Not to do so would indicate an air of authority or superiority over the person being called or beckoned.

Like many in Asia, the Vietnamese are an extremely superstitious people. Ancestry and the direct link to the spirit world of the beyond are not mere intangibles in Vietnam, but daily occurrences and as such must be treated with respect, dignity, and above all, caution!

For instance, you should never touch anyone on the head, as this would be considered as a personal insult to the individual and perhaps even to his ancestors. Many Vietnamese believe the spirit resides there. Hence, the belief that if a person is beheaded, his spirit will roam forever without finding a resting place.

Also, as hard as it may be to resist, don't touch anyone on the shoulder. Some people believe that a genie resides there and it is undesirable to disturb him. If you mistakenly touch one on his or her shoulder, you must also touch the other shoulder as this helps offset the bad luck.

Vietnamese people have a habit of not looking into your eyes when they talk to you. In America this would be considered rude, but in Vietnam it is in fact quite the opposite. This is often because

22   Hgoc, H., Sketches for a Portrait of Vietnamese Culture (Hanoi, The Global Publishers) 1995

of shyness, but one of the main reasons is that traditionally they do not look into the eyes of those they respect or those higher in rank when talking to them. This is to indicate politeness.

The smile of a Vietnamese can be very confusing to an outsider in Vietnam and occasionally even cause misunderstandings. In some Asian countries, a smile can mean sorrow, worry, or embarrassment. In Vietnam, it may indicate a polite, but perhaps skeptical reaction to something, compliance or toleration of a blunder or misunderstanding or, on occasion, represents submission to judgment that may be wrong or unfair.

This is particularly true if the one making the judgment is at a superior level and perhaps has lost his temper. For instance, a laundress may ruin a favorite shirt and is called in by her employer to be asked about it. In turn, she may smile. This does not mean that she thinks it is funny that she burned the shirt, but instead is an unspoken submission to the fact. If the owner of the shirt loses his temper, she may in fact *keep* smiling, indicating politeness or patience with her superiors.

Because of this, foreigners should be very cautious in voicing their opinions and perhaps be a little more delicate, more tolerant, and certainly should try to refrain from being obstinate.

Loud arguments or heated discussions are frowned upon and are seldom heard among the Vietnamese. Well-bred people are trained in self-discipline. It is best for foreigners to do their best to keep tempers in check, no matter what the circumstances, lest they be looked upon with disdain.

Vietnamese seldom use a direct approach in their dealings. To do so indicates a lack of tact or delicacy. Directness is appreciated in the Western world, but not in Vietnam. The Vietnamese do not like to say "no" and will often reply "yes" when the answer should be negative. This problem is further complicated by Americans posing negative questions such as, "It doesn't look like it will rain today, does it?" The correct answer is often the one given by the Vietnamese: "Yes." However, we expect to hear "No."

Think it out, though, and you will see that the Vietnamese is really correct.

Best advice, don't ask negative questions.

The Lucky 13:

A Baker's Dozen of Irl's Good Advice

These customs and compromises are a lot to remember, I know. Worse yet, it's just like learning a foreign language: Unless you use it, you'll lose it. I can speak confidently of the cultural differences between Vietnam and America, as well as the various subtle nuances that can hamper, or help, a business negotiation, because I've seen them firsthand and experienced them for myself.

But rest easy: Here I've compiled a baker's dozen of the most confusing (to us anyway) and cherished (to the Vietnamese) customs that were destined to trip you up somewhere along the way. I say "were" because, after reading them, your ability to deal with the Vietnamese will make such social blunders a thing of the past:

1. Don't express lavish admiration for a new baby, because the devils might hear you and steal the child because of his or her desirability.

2. When going somewhere on business, avoid seeing a woman first. If you *do* see a woman first as you go out your door or on the way, postpone the trip.

3. Mirrors are often placed on front doors. Why? Simple, really: If a dragon tries to get in, he will see his reflection and think that there is already a dragon there and go away.

4. Single bowls of rice and chopsticks should not be served. Always place at least two on a table. One bowl is for the dead. Never let chopsticks touch others or make unnecessary noise with them. Do not place chopsticks in food and leave them there.

5. Do not hand someone a toothpick.

6. Never buy one pillow or mattress pad, always buy two.

7. Do not use relative's towels.

8. Do not overturn musical instruments, or beat both sides of a drum simultaneously.

9. Do not cut finger and toenails at night.

10. Going Dutch, a popular American pastime, with a Vietnamese is *not* appreciated. If you run into someone at a restaurant and you join his table, let him pay the whole bill or pay it all yourself. When in doubt, remember: The senior person usually pays.

11. Gifts for brides and grooms are usually given in pairs, including blankets. A single item indicates the marriage is not expected to last long. Two less expensive items are more desirable than one nicer one.

12. Educated people and others who are not in the peasant class do not work with their hands. To do so would appear to try to beat a poor peasant out of his job. In addition, it is considered beneath the dignity of refined people.

13. Hats are not usually worn inside churches, even Catholic ones.

THE FINAL WORD?

Realizing that a lack of information about different cultures and their business practices has doomed the efforts of many international businesses, it is very important that we understand the differences in doing business in the West and doing business in Vietnam.

Every person who is planning to open a business in the country must look at the cultural differences of the country they are thinking of operating in. Keeping our awareness to these differences must be, at all times, in the front of our negotiations so that cultural ignorance does not become synonymous with professional ignorance.

The deepening of the western economic, commercial, and assistance relationship with Vietnam will eventually promote civil society, encourage economic reform, draw the country further into the rules-based international trading system, and promote interests of the western business person. Until then, it is our duty to understand Vietnam in order to do business there.

As the Japanese business person we shared such a pleasant business meeting with declared, "In the future, the eyes of the west will rest on Vietnam as a co-creative partner."

Vietnam is starting to interest many global businesses.

How about yours?

INTERACTING WITH KOREA – THE FORGING OF AN INTERNATIONAL BUSINESSMAN 5

When I initially began my path on the road to becoming an international businessman, one of the first countries I stepped into was South Korea. Now, this country may not be as instantly recognizable to you as, say, China or Japan, but as we all know in business some of the best bets fly well under the competition's radar. During the early 1980's, for instance, when I was beginning to expand my operations overseas, South Korea offered a diverse business community that gave my company a definite edge in an increasingly competitive market.

As always, you should have a specific goal in mind when touring another country. For me, the primary reason for visiting South Korea at that time was to evaluate a manufacturing facility that was recommended by a business friend of mine who had previous experience doing business with the Koreans. (Remember: It never hurts to have a trusted friend go through the experience before you. They often do you the additional favor of working out the kinks before you get on board!)

In order to fully understand the significant experience I gained in South Korea, and the reason why this volume centers around those in the Asian community, the reader must first understand some of the many cultural characteristics that the Koreans share with the Chinese and Japanese. This is primarily due to the long history of contact Korea has had with these countries, as well as its geographic proximity to them. Actually, China was the primary birthing culture for the Koreans.

The prospective businessperson must also understand that a significant part of the Korean character was forged by bloody, on-going battles with invaders from the sea and the north (basically every corner of the globe).

There are hundreds of books written by scholars, psychologists, businessmen and others striving to explain the mind-set and behavior of the Korean people since the early nineteenth century, and with good reason: Few nations have been under siege as often and from as many foreign invaders as Korea has.

It is not necessary to read every book about Korea to do business there, but I *do* believe that understanding some of the Korean language and its key words can provide valuable insight into the Korean mind; their emotions, concepts, and attitudes. Not only will gaining a better cultural understanding of the Korean people help you understand them, it will also inform you how to go about doing business with them.

I was very lucky to gain a mentor and develop a friendship with a Korean professor. He was instrumental in developing my sensitivity to both the Korean culture and to the mind-set of its people, as well as an ongoing understanding of the subtleties of the Korean language.

In all my years of traveling abroad and doing business with those who dress, act, eat, drink, and speak differently than myself, I can honestly say that few cultures weigh their words as significantly as the Korean people do. Words are not just language to the Koreans, they are an art form. After five years of continual business with the Koreans, I have the greatest appreciation of the culture-laden words in the Korean language.

It is interesting to note that the majority of the Koreans share only four to five family names (in Western terms; your last name). There is an abundance of "Kim's" and "Park's" in Korea, but please don't confuse this with "keeping up with the Joneses." Subtlety is everything in Korea; it is important for the western businessperson to distinguish the difference.

BEFORE THE FOREIGNER

If language is a Korean art form, than history is the canvas across which the Korean mindset is splashed. Koreans are a vibrant and colorful people, but their character and pride go far beyond the typical Asian stereotype. Dates and facts are one thing, but doing business in Korea demands a certain sensitivity to history that goes beyond the Cliff Notes version.

It is important to know some history of Korea and the pre-modern Korean society as it is the basis of much of the business behavior you will eventually observe. Though I was not as familiar with its history when I first visited Korea as I am now, from years of research I would consider the Chinese to be the first foreigner to put their feet in Korea, about 4,000 years ago.

For the next 3,500 years Korea was invaded by the Japanese, the Mongols, as well as the Chinese. It wasn't until around the sixteenth century when the first westerner showed his face in Korea. In fact, following an invasion by Japan around 1592-1598 (and another one by the Manchurians in the 1630's) Korea closed its doors to *all* outsiders. [23]

It wasn't until the early 1600's that a Dutchman showed up, given a military post *and* a Korean name (he was an expert in fire-arms), and married a Korean girl. To put it in a literary perspective, he was the Korean version of James Clavell's *Shogun*.

---

23 United States Central Intelligent Agency, The World Fact Book (U.S. Government) 2004

By 1832 an increasing number of merchant ships and warships showed up in the Korean waters, and it's clear to see why this vibrant, rich, and vast coastal country became the target for such ongoing aggression.

Up to this time, I am amazed at how many military conflicts this country endured (some of its own making). As a result of this constant defense of their territory, I believe that the military and war strategy is ingrained into the language and culture.

Bypassing some interesting historical conflicts, Korea was finally forced to open its doors to westerners in 1876.[24] As a result, a massive tidal wave of missionaries, educators and professionals soon rushed to Korea. Not surprisingly, Japan jumped into Korea and installed a puppet ruler in 1895. Korean rebels later attacked the occupational forces. Japan retaliated and eventually annexed Korea, thereby eliminating it as a national entity. Over the next 35 years Japan attempted to obliterate the national and cultural identity of all Koreans. They weren't alone: During this difficult time the Japanese kicked out all the westerners, thereby cutting Korea off from the outside world.

It's not surprising that the Korean experience with foreigners throughout its history was very unpleasant and insulting and even destructive on a massive scale. (To read how the Koreans have been oppressed for centuries, you can obtain some of these stories for yourself at your local library.)

In order to understand the Korean businessman you *must* grasp the notion that words are not just words, but instead have a "rank," or strict position of importance, to Koreans. During my early times in Korea my mentor had his "top-ten" listed and made me repeat them until I knew them by heart. He felt that knowledge of cultural words was one of the keys to opening the door of success in Korea.

He was right ...

Most of these rankings are based upon obvious reasons: When an entire country must watch its every word so as not to offend,

---

24   United States Central Intelligent Agency, The World Fact Book (U.S. Government) 2004

or inform, an occupying force, words truly do become "weapons." The reader must acknowledge that there actually IS a ranking rather than just a form of grammar or structure to the language. This ranking is culturally related and I find it is based on an ancient Confucian fact.

Whoever you talk to about this subject will have some opinions about the rankings themselves, but they all agree that such words have an importance beyond their literal meaning. Nevertheless, there is a rank.

For conversation's sake, some of the words that find its way to the top-ten are: Father, Son, Mother, study, and money. One can certainly argue about the other words, but let's concentrate on these to show how significant such "simple" words can be to the Korean culture.

The relationship between mother and father (and their children) has changed dramatically throughout Korea's turbulent history. The difference between generations often occurs gradually over time, but with a history as violent and turbulent as Korea's, the cultural divide occurred within one generation. None was more apparent than during the student riots of the late 1980's.

Yours truly just happened to have a front row seat to this debacle; I watched out the window of the Hilton hotel, where I was staying, while the police formed a ring around the church where students were holing up after their marching protest against what they felt was the outdated and tyrannical rule of their parents' generation.

Tension was in the air as our quaint little downtown district suddenly became ground zero for what was to become an international incident. The sounds of marching shoulders and war machines thundered down the street. As pepper gas was sprayed and my fellow hotel guests and I caught wind of it, I was harshly reminded of the cultural differences that were dividing the students, who were eager to be free of the bonds of their strict cultural upbringing, and their families, who were desperately clinging to the safety and security of "the old ways."

The students were being taught by missionaries and professors and exchange students the western methods while their immediate families were entrenched in the older cultural values that had seen them triumph over foreign invaders for the entirety of their country's history. This dichotomy, this culture clash, if you will, only deepened the divide between the children and their families.

The conflict I witnessed that day was its direct result.

During the 1970's the much-coveted "good-life" for a typical Korean was plentiful food, clothing, and electronic gadgets. By the end of the 1980's all of that had changed. Now ordinary people were able to indulge themselves with many material things. It was the beginning of the age of affluence, as well as much of Korea's internal strife between its warring generations.

This age was known as the Orange Group (the Korean version of the X or Y generation). Although there are some negative connotations attached with the Orange Group (affluence) it will certainly fade as the 21st Century Korea rises to a position of prominence in the international community.

What makes the Korea of today easier to work with than the Korea of, say, the 1990's is their desire and drive toward "globalization" or what they call *Segyehwa* (say-gay-hwah). Fortunately for us, this globalization is a state of mind that is becoming prevalent in South Korea. Universities and top executives are using this word as it's a condition they are striving to access with more relation to foreign markets.

What does this all mean to you? All of this is great news to the international business that is considering Korea as a fertile land of opportunity. Want more great news (and perhaps a little reassurance that you don't have to learn Korean before doing business there)? Even top executives in Korea are insisting that the day-to-day business in their international departments be conducted in English. This good news must not make the westerner overconfident. It will, however, allow a much easier bridge to the Korean markets.

As the years have passed, so has Korea's resolve to fear foreigners less, and do business with them more often. As a result, the "new" Korea is becoming stronger and stronger with each passing year. Even with the economic stress of the late 1990's, Korea is emerging as a great opportunity for the international businessperson.

BUT FIRST ...

A Little Background

The story is as old as the country: Historically speaking, South Korea's economy has always been based on agriculture but the entire culture has undergone an extraordinarily rapid industrialization ever since the early 1960s. As a result, the country's gross domestic product (GDP) expanded by more than nine percent annually between the mid-1960s and mid-1990s. Thanks to this learning curve, Korea can now compete industrially with many of its Asian counterparts.

Powers that be spotted the trend, and pledged to continue it: A series of five-year economic plans implemented beginning in 1962 concentrated on the development of export-oriented and import-substituting manufacturing. Economic aid, especially from the superpowers of United States and Japan, has been vital to the economic growth of the country, which in the span of a single generation grew from one of the world's poorest nations to what it is today: a major industrial power.

As one of the "Four Dragons" of East Asia – alongside such rivals as Taiwan, Singapore, and Hong Kong – South Korea has achieved an incredible record of expansion during its relatively short time on the playing field of international commerce. Three decades ago, its GDP per capita was comparable to the poorer countries of Africa and Asia. Today (2004), its GDP per capita is seven times India's, 13 times North Korea's and already close to that of the lower ranking economies of the European Union.[25]

This success through the late 1980s was achieved by a system of close ties between government and business, including directed credit, import restrictions, sponsorship of specific industries and a strong labor effort.

---

25 United States Central Intelligent Agency, The World Fact Book (U.S. Government) 2004

The government promoted the import of raw materials and technology at the expense of consumer goods and encouraged savings and investment over consumption. Under this development regime, South Korean business groups grew into large multinational enterprises, but there was also a tendency for each major group to mirror what the others were doing and to push growth at the expense of profitability and sound balance sheets.

By the mid-1990s, while some business were large, there was considerable duplication in their output mix (e.g. most groups were in automobile manufacturing) and a growing overhang of excess capacity that required more and more export volume to keep the factories busy.

Meanwhile, the standard of living was rising rapidly; a prosperous middle class was rapidly emerging and as a result spending on consumer goods, including imports from other countries, was rising rapidly. In fact, by the mid-1990s, the "export dependent" Korean economy was actually running merchandise trade deficits and by 1996, the current account deficit had ballooned to more than US $23 billion, or 4.5 percent of Korea's GDP.

The Asian financial crisis of 1997-1998 exposed long-standing weaknesses in South Korea's development model, including high corporate debt-equity ratios, massive foreign borrowing and an undisciplined financial sector in which lending liberally supported headlong industrial expansion without due regard for profitability.

While South Korea was affected by the global economic slowdown of 2001, it weathered the storm much better than many of its middle-income export-oriented neighbors, who suffered the inevitable recessions when the United States economy slowed. Meanwhile, Korea's GDP grew 3.0 percent. And, in 2002, despite a still stagnant global economy, South Korea grew very strongly at 6.1 percent, one of the best performances of any country in the OECD.

Now you can see why a country like Korea rates its own chapter here ...

"TO-DOG OR NOT-TO- DOG"

THAT is the Question!

Personally speaking, I have discovered that Koreans divide foreigners into two separate and distinct categories (a) have they ever been to Korea before (b) do they have any "connections." The more connections you have the better the typical Korean businessperson will accept you. Even when it comes to connections, Koreans have a different take on things. Where westerners often prize business connections over the academic or personal, some of the most meaningful connections, according to Koreans, including having experience teaching at a Korean University, studied at a Korean University and/or if you are related by blood or marriage.

Therefore, to most of us, experience is the craft we must develop if we want to compete effectively with our Korean counterparts. If you are not in the best category and you are just getting some experience, don't expect huge success with the first or second visit. Still, don't let that get in the way of at least trying. You may not make much headway, but simply having your foot in the door of this ground floor opportunity is worth the lumps you might take gaining that experience for your next visit.

As I have said, Koreans want our business. At the same time, they're not going to hand it over without a few tests first. As a part of this "feeling out" process, I found that the Koreans will traditionally measure the "commitment" that foreigners may or may not have to Korea in a variety of, let's just say … challenging … ways.

One of these is taking you to a "dog meat" restaurant ...

Let us not blanch at this thought at first blush, but instead consider the fact that *Posintang* (poh-sint-ahing) is a traditional dish in Korea and is considered for its health-giving characteristics.

I was subjected to this "test" early in the 1980's. Here is where your upbringing can make or break you: As for myself, I was fortunate enough to have been raised on a farm in central Oregon where we, like most farmers, "raised-what-we-ate." On the farm we were taught early on to eat what is given to us, and not complain, be it a meal of calf's liver, prairie dog, or rattlesnake.

All of this allowed me to enjoy the food as it was prepared that fateful night I first enjoyed the traditional Korean meal of Posintang. It should be noted that the Koreans can be humorous at times with Posintang, particularly when they are entertaining westerners they know are tasting it for the first time, but they take it very seriously.

In earlier chapters I've talked about the "when in Rome" concept. Nowhere is it more important in Korea than when it comes to the dinner table. Groaning, rolling one's eyes, pretending to be full, denying a host's offer or turning up one's nose as the meal is prepared will definitely sour an otherwise profitable deal.

The rewards of enjoying such a meal can be plentiful: I must say that once my Korean hosts observed me enjoying the dish and drinking the soju they offered, I was immediately declared to have been a "Korean" in a previous life and it was obviously continuing today in my spirit.

The outside world was not as understanding as I was, or so it seemed, about the health benefits of Posintang: As you may recall, 1988 was the time of the summer Olympics in South Korea. A lot of animal-right advocates (who were in town from all over the world) made such a fuss about eating dog that the government ordered the restaurants that served such Korean delicacies "shut down." I use quotes around the term because what actually happened was that the restaurants didn't close down; instead they just changed their signs.

During this brief period I was visiting Seoul and one evening found myself heading for my favorite Posintang restaurant with five other Koreans from the factory I was visiting at the time.

Like many Asian countries Korea is known for its vast population and cramped conditions, so noise and crowds and congestion are old hat for me by this point. I was also used to being accepted, but the Olympics and the eyes of the world had changed all that. At least for one eventful night in the quest for Posintang.

Approaching the restaurant I noticed the typical loud talking and laughing from about 50 patrons of the restaurant. It was always an "event" for me to discuss business with the Koreans, as in any typical restaurant, bar, or gathering place you are surrounded by loud, familiar, boisterous, and very vocal patrons, and this event seemed no different from the rest.

Once we stepped inside the loud restaurant, however, it suddenly became very silent. I was stunned. All eyes were on me, the only westerner in the facility. Even the servers stood still. I never felt so obvious, or out of place, in my life. Flanked by five Koreans we made it to the only vacant table and it wasn't until I stood up and toasted my fellow Koreans with Soju that the noise returned to its normal, ear defining, levels. (Never had such an orgy of sound been such music to my ears.)

Once I started to eat the Posintang other Koreans got into the festive mood and by the time we left (some three deafening hours later) our eyes were blurry with Soju and my humble group of friends had increased from five to fifty.

The moral to this story is not that you should be forced to eat dog meat if you are politically, physically, socially, morally, or simply digestively opposed to it. The moral is that you should never forget that you are a guest on foreign soil and that foreigners have customs, rituals, and even dishes that must be respected.

As a foreign businessperson, if you are subjected to this test you need to be very, very diplomatic if you choose to refrain from eating dog meat. The best way to salvage the awkward situation is simply to apologize (smiling all the while) and explain quite respectfully if forcefully that it is "against your religious beliefs." A spiritual people themselves, your Korean hosts may not follow your belief, but they will at least be respectful and understanding.

THE OLD SONG AND DANCE, OR:

Drinking and Singing Your Way to the Business Deal

You've heard of singing for your supper? Well, I think that's a Korean "dogma" that somehow got lost in translation! As a businessperson in Korea, you will be challenged to participate in another local custom of *norae* (singing). Actually, this is no new song and dance: solo singing in Korea finds it roots around 1,000 BC. It was common for local tribes to sit around a campfire and sing to the visiting tribe. Obviously, this was long before karaoke was introduced by the Japanese in the 1970's.

Karaoke swept most of the world in the 1980's. Even westerners are now getting into the swing of solo singing in front of a crowd of people, though it's yet to become a part of most western business meals. The Japanese word *karaoke* actually means "empty orchestra." This term is actually quite reminiscent to me holding a tune (actually it refers to the singers performing to recorded music and not with live musicians, but it's hard not to take the term personally with a voice like mine).

To a Korean, the singing and drinking clubs in which they prefer to do business provide a powerful bonding experience that is necessary for close relationships, be they personal or professional. Koreans consider this method of relationships building very important to the businessman, so if you've already decided against dining on Posintang, you better at least agree to eat some crow and take to the microphone if you want to avoid having two strikes against you instead of one.

It may seem daunting, but there are ways to soften the blow if you are overly nervous, or under qualified, to sing on stage. For instance, if you cannot hold a tune then get some of your Korean friends up on the stage with you. Far from being offended, they will be delighted to sing as a group.

Singing and drinking are equally important to the relationships that are required by the typical Korean businessperson. How one conducts himself (or herself) during this time is important to your success. Drinking can be conducted in moderation. However, there will be many toasts and conversation that will revolve around the business (a toast of congratulations) and to the future (a toast to our continued prosperity) and your time in Korea (you get the picture).

So forget those charts and graphs you spent hours pouring over, keeping your wits about you will sometimes be the most challenging aspect of a typical Korean business lunch or dinner.

I got what you might call some firsthand experience with this particular Korean pastime sometime during 1987. A friend of mine was working for a company who was looking for specific product to import to the USA. During one of my visits to Korea, my friend decided to take the same route as I was to share the journey.

Often, we attempted to coordinate our trips to travel together but it didn't always work out. Normally we would travel alone and on long trips, unless it was more effective to travel the same route. By traveling together we would share information and give one another time to brainstorm with another westerner. It provided a great way to ensure our visits were highly effective, and it didn't hurt to feel like we were "home away from home" for each other for a week or two.

This particular trip would end up to be a close ending of our relationship, but a great lesson on what not to do in a Korean business drinking session.

First a little background on Korean business drinking: Historically, drinking in Korea began as a religious ritual. I believe it was easier to communicate with their gods when one was in a drunken state. Then during the form of Confucianism (an influence straight from China) the role of women became totally subservient to men. Drinking by women was strictly prohibited. Therefore drinking became an exclusive activity for men. I believe there was a method to their madness: The reason for the popularity of male only drinking, apparently, was that they could now ignore (or at least avoid) the more formal behavior they had formerly had to put on display when females were present and act "more normal." (Talk about letting your hair down!)

When modernization – and hordes of foreign businesspeople – at last came to Korea, drinking was perhaps inevitably incorporated into the business methods as an important part of relationship building. This included both inside the company (employee to employee) but with other businesses (CEO to CEO) as well. Therefore, business drinking became an integrated element of Korean society.

It serves several purposes: When drinking the Korean can complain loudly, be informal, and even shout at their superiors. (Just try *that* at the IBM ice cream social next year!) This can be a bonding ritual for the Korean business person. In a normal setting Korean culture does not allow for such intimacy or openness.

Now it might be more apparent to you why the foreigner must take Korean business drinking very seriously. Although drinking socially and professionally can be considered beneficial for the same purpose, it's the Korean business drinking that serves a higher degree of importance with the business person.

And thus it should with you, as well …

With this in mind, back to the story: I was concluding my visit with one of the Korean factories that represented about 30% of my business at the time. We had just completed a very successful process of negotiation that would eventually lead into a substantial growth for both of us.

To celebrate, and finalize the deal, five of my Korean friends and I were heading out for an evening of traditional drinking and singing, ala Korean business and social customs. My friend had just happened to finish up his visit early and was patiently waiting for mine to conclude as we were flying to Taipei together the next day. Naturally, I invited my friend along for the drinking and singing and to celebrate my success.

Our evening started out at a local bar known as a Norae Bang (singing salon). During the day most Korean businessmen are very serious and extremely work-oriented. Most are not given any levity or toleration to frivolous behavior at their workplaces. Behind their face of formality and obsessive ambition, however, is a fun-loving person trying to get out and play. As I have seen in recent years, they certainly find their way out at the Norae Bang or Kisaeng (hostess-stocked cabarets).

Unlike typical western karaoke bars, which are heavy on the audience participation and light on such private moments, Norae Bangs and Kisaeng's have private rooms serviced by beautiful young ladies that serve exotic food and drinks and provide companionship to the lonely singer. There is nothing untoward about the arrangement, these are not the champagne rooms typified by American men's clubs, but instead these private rooms serve all kinds of drinks, food and provide a safe, casual, and stress-free environment in which the local businessperson can enjoy himself.

Here we find my friend, five Koreans, and I in a room made for half that amount of people. The Kisaeng was not in the most prominent area and certainly not of the caliber you would recommend to your mother if she were taking her church group to visit Korea. Everyone smoked and the drinks were flowing. Hostesses were cycled on a constant basis to ensure the consumption of Soju was at the level which would ensure the utmost profitability for the coming week.

Celebration was in order, not just for those who had successfully engaged in the positive negotiations but, it seemed, for everyone (including the owner of the Kisaeng). Innocently enough, my friend began drinking Soju to join in the celebration.

There are many types of Soju in Korea and the particular type I drink is more commonly found in the rustic areas of Korea. It usually takes two drinks to "deaden the taste buds" before you can begin toasting your Korean counterpart. Once you begin drinking this popular local libation, it is highly advisable not to drink anything else. (Kind of like mixing tequila with vodka. Sounds good on paper, looks bad on the porcelain!)

As the evening developed my friend began, with the ribald and enthusiastic encouragement of our hosts, to mix Soju with American liquor. As the evening came to an end, I began to search for my friend, who was no longer in sight. After some brief inquiries I was directed to a local, communal, bathroom.

This story might have resolved itself quite differently had we been back in America. But to quote Judy Garland, we sure weren't back in Kansas anymore. To most westerners, the sight of a Korean bathroom is both shocking and confusing when they first encounter one. Most rural bathrooms consist of a simple hole in the floor in which a stream of water constantly moves the waste to somewhere .... unknown. Bathrooms that are more "upscale" may consist of a porcelain hole in the floor. However, many hotels now are fitted with the latest "johns" that are more familiar with western operation.

Unfortunately, we were not in a hotel

GEORGE HELPS TO INDOCTRINATE ME INTO BUSINESS-NEGOTIATION-KOREAN-STYLE

Thus the search for my friend found him on the floor of one such rural bathroom. A few of the bathroom patrons – including my five Korean friends who had joined me during my search – were standing around watching this curious westerner make use of the facilities in a very un-businesslike manner. To say the least, my Korean business friends were not too impressed with my friend and his "business-etiquette." (Or lack thereof.) As we have read previously, it is important to remember that most Koreans will "test" foreigners. This is both with song as well as the drink.

It is also important to understand what signals we are sending to our Korean partners, as well to develop an ability to "receive" these signals. Most Koreans that I have developed this type of friendship with state that most foreigners never "understand them." I think if we listened more, and drank less, we might understand them a whole lot better.

After that fateful night, my friend was ill for two days. To this day, the word Soju will make him physically, visibly ill. Of course, though we continue to be close, he no longer travels with me.

NORTH, SOUTH, EAST, WEST:

The Global Squeeze Play

South Korea's relationship with North Korea has been one of the key current political issues dominating the past century. In 1992, an accord was signed stipulating non-aggression, reconciliation, and cooperative exchanges between North and South Korea. Meanwhile, impoverished North Korea has been the recipient of humanitarian aid from South Korea, despite the prevailing hostilities between the two entities.[26]

The major aspects of the accord involve the reunification of estranged families who have been divided by the political fate of the peninsula, and more abstract arenas of reconciliation, cooperation, a climate of entente, and the long-term possibility of reunification. It was hoped that this kind of substantive engagement could be realized by separating business from politics, and by emphasizing the shared ideals designated in the 1992 accord.

---

26 United States Central Intelligent Agency, The World Fact Book (U.S. Government) 2004

In early 2000, the world saw the two Koreas take a big step toward the desired goal of rapprochement. The two Koreas announced in April that a summit would be held between the top leaders of both Koreas in Pyongyang. South Korean President Kim Dae-jung's "sunshine policy" of engagement with North Korea had contributed significantly to the mutual agreement of holding a summit. Economic reforms and reconciliation with North Korea have been the two core policies of the Kim government.

One of the primary technologies that will dissolve constraints between countries and is becoming a major boon to the global manager is satellite television. I believe this is the beginning of the "death of distance." Beginning in the 1980's and accelerating into the 21st century, it will help develop the need to teleconference between countries.

Broadcasters are arguing that the model is a common language which will begin to prevail and all political differences will begin to shrink. I am not of the opinion that TV broadcasting will be, in itself, the savior of future political conflicts. However, it certainly will assist the business person in exposure to other cultures and accelerate teleconferencing to the point where distance no longer becomes an excuse for delaying meetings, or the resolutions that might eventually come from them.

The popularization of the fax machine in the early 1980's brought a communication boon to the small businessperson. No longer did foreign recipients need to translate typed text spewing out of the old teletype machine. Today, the fax allows the sharing of symbols, drawings and visual forms of expression that crossed the language barrier and expanded our global horizons.

This was truly the birth of "practical" globalization, and its ramifications for the future of doing business abroad are truly rippling through the world. Teleconferencing, or the merging of live video over the internet, will be another leap into the next century with globalization. Meetings can (and will one day) be common across cultural borders, be they right next door or thousands of miles away. Live translation software is already being experimented with and used in some isolated areas. Once these types of technologies become available to the small professional like you and I, great leaps will occur in global management.

This technology, however, will bring on other opportunities to the global manager as well. The reasoning behind why companies and markets differ should be thought of not on one dimension, but in its multidimensionality. There is no "one-answer" to cross-cultural marketplaces anymore, nor is there one "proper" style of global management. In fact, any book published prior to 2000 that is based upon opinion (versus statistics) needs to be rewritten, up-dated, and republished within a few short years.

Communication technology is accelerating *that* fast.

The point to this discussion is to apprise the reader that the Koreans are aware of this fact. English is being taught at all school levels. Satellite broadcasting emphasizes the diverse languages that are as close as the channel button on your remote. This is giving way to the necessity of a common language within the global business arena.

While in Korea my good friend (the university professor in Seoul) remarked about Wal-Mart. One of the decisions that kept Wal-Mart successful, particularly as they expanded into global territories where travel costs can be prohibitive, was they kept expenses low, not just in their stores, but behind the scenes, all the way from shipping and distribution to employee expense accounts. They demanded that trip expenses were carefully managed. Even executives shared rooms with other employees while traveling and walked instead of taking a taxi.

My professor friend felt that reducing travel expenses was driving the desire for teleconferencing more than ever before. If broadcast television made us aware of the language difference, they also made us aware of the shrinking global distances. Much like travel allowed us to communicate with each other in the past, modern technology will soon allow us to communicate over this shirking bridge.

The Koreans are also considering the avenue of least differences. The successful Korean business is now strategizing for the midrange in which cultural barriers between countries are neither so large as to effectively isolate them nor so negligible that they are not expanding. Under this consideration, North Korea is a large potential market for the South Koreans.

The Train Trip of Loyalty:

"Songshilhan"

By now you've heard several of my travel stories, and I hope you've learned from them. I know I certainly have. While many of my travels aboard allow for pleasure trips, it is rare that I don't learn something about the country I'm visiting from the places in which I'm vacationing.

Case in point: Once I was in Seoul on business over a weekend and wanted to see the country and some of the interesting sites during my down time. My Korean friend invited me to go with him and his girlfriend on a 4-hour train ride to southern Korea to visit a temple located there. I was quite excited about his invitation, not only for the opportunity to explore but also that my personal relationship with an important businessman was developing.

The train system in Korea is very good and extremely organized. Color coded to the "class" of ticket, we soon found ourselves en route to the southern tip of Korea. Crossing beautiful, fertile farm land and many villages the scenery was worth the price of admission in and of itself. To someone who had been landlocked by high rises and karaoke bars for much of my visit, it was as much exciting as it was beautiful.

The arrival of the train found beautiful weather and the temple was, in fact, in the midst of a vibrant and historically rich celebration to honor an ancient General. What was interesting about this historical figure was his demand of loyalty within his troops.

The Korean society is one which personal relationships define and control virtually all behavior. Loyalty becomes one of the primary pillars of every aspect of Korean life. This, of course, is a bit dangerous as it is ruled by emotions and not principles.

After a full day at this temple, my host and his lovely girlfriend guided me back to the train only to find the last train leaving for the day. It was so crowed that people were handing out of the windows, doors, and from any bar they could grab. For someone used to the western mode of public transportation, and not so used to it as business grew as I was when business was poor, it was amazing to see this spectacle of man and machine.

At this time in Korea there were no taxi cabs that could travel from one end of Korea to another. Therefore, we were forced to take a taxi from one village to the next, quickly pay and disembark and then flag another to do the same routine all over again. It took us over 12 hours to get home.

All was not lost, however: During this taxi cab marathon my friend explained to me the importance of loyalty for the Korean businessperson: In pre-modern Korea, loyalty (called *songshilhan*) was focused on one's family or equated to inferiors obeying superiors without questions (therefore the suggested visit to the general's temple, which had obviously been offered by my business acquaintance to illustrate the importance of our two companies' loyalty to each other).

Loyalty in present day Korea is still more people-oriented but has transitioned to loyalty to, and between, companies. In companies and other places of employment, individual Koreans have attached themselves to either managers who had power or were clearly on the "advancement elevator." By demonstrating absolute loyalty to these managers they made themselves indispensable and were thus inevitably "pulled up" by the manager as he or she advanced through the ranks of the company. This kind of loyalty actually took precedence over raw talent until the late 1980's and early 1990's.

Today personal loyalty remains an overridingly important characteristic in Korea. In fact, once a business starts doing business with another company the loyalty becomes even more important. Once you begin doing business it is very difficult to break off the relationship. Unlike in America, where competition is embraced, doing business with more than one company is a very sensitive matter and may be regarded as "not showing respect (i.e. loyalty) for the other company."

Koreans can get upset by foreign companies coming in and "shopping around" for better prices, better agents, different partners and approaching different companies at the same time. This is an important fact to remember, especially since westerners often do business this way. But remember: What's common back home could be highly offensive in Korea, and many of the other Asian cultures we've discussed, so use the travel time over to put yourself in the mindset "the western way is not always the right way."

Simple efforts can go a long way in helping you do business with a modern Korean company. I suggest reading up on their food – tastes, habits, culture, etc. – and some other items to remember can go a long way toward blending in more quickly and doing business more efficiently. Here are a few of them:

- Saving "face" is more important than truth or honesty. Don't damage anyone's emotions in public.

- Remember, making a friend is more important than "making the deal."

- Koreans tend to be more emotional than logical. As a result, the processes are usually more important than the end result.

- Know the position of the people you are talking to ... check the name card; it will show you everything you need to know about their position. Always talk to the highest position available.

- Negotiation is everything. Koreans love to do it and are good at it. Brinkmanship is an art form. Learn it.

- Face-to-face meetings are more important than email or formal letters.

- Koreans are hesitant to ask for clarification if they don't understand you. Make sure they do.

- Adapt to the culture. (Both with food and their manner.) It will carry you a long way.

- Don't let it show that time is a factor in your negotiations.

- Know the proper way to address the senior managers.[27]

CULTURAL DO'S & DON'TS

Finally, remember at all times that *you* are the guest in Korea, and not the other way around. It's easy to lapse into being the "ugly American," often without even knowing it; so know it!

As westerners we often feel superior to the cultures we visit (witness our emblematic revulsion to the typical Korean toilet), but we can learn a lot about a culture, and how they do business, by reserving judgment and simply pushing pause on our American button until we're back on our home turf.

I'm not saying don't be yourself; you'll never do honest business that way. What I am saying is to listen more than you talk, observe more than you act out, and before you do anything, reflect on whether or not it might offend those you're doing business with.

I know; it's not always easy to tell what will offend someone from a different culture. But learn from my mistakes, and memorize the following cultural do's and don'ts when visiting Korea. They could just be a lifesaver:

- Korean men tend to greet each other with a slight bow, sometimes accompanied by a handshake, while maintaining eye contact. In order to indicate respect for the person being greeted, one might support one's right forearm with one's left hand during the handshake.

---

27   KTNET, Korean Culture (The Trade Automation Service) 1991

- Elderly people are very highly respected in Korean culture and, as such, it is customary in group settings to greet and speak to them first, taking care to spend a few moments with them before turning your attention toward your younger business acquaintance.

- Travelers should be aware that Korean males possess higher social status than Korean women. Although Western women are excluded from these rules, *all* travelers should be aware of this cultural difference and should not show that they are offended by it.

- In South Korea, physical contact is inappropriate with older people, with people of the opposite sex, or with people who are not good friends and family.

- Koreans are restrained and self-possessed people; travelers should avoid being loud and boisterous around them. (Until, that is, you get to the karaoke bar!)

- When in South Korea, one should cover your mouth when yawning or using toothpicks.

- Likewise, blowing one's nose in public is considered bad manners.

- As in many Asian cultures, smiling and laughter does not always denote amusement and pleasure; smiling and laughter can just as easily denote discomfort. For example, when a typical Korean is embarrassed, he or she may laugh excessively. Learn to spot the difference.

- Koreans are very conscious of dignity and self-respect. As in other parts of eastern Asia, "protecting face" is a very important and delicate concern. One should never embarrass another person, especially in public.

- Modesty is another cardinal concern in Korea. One should not enter a home or office until one is invited to do so, and one should not sit down unless one has been asked to take a seat.

- When offering compliments about someone's belongings, one should take care not to be overly-appreciative as good manner suggests that they would then be obligated to give it to you.

- One should not visit a Korean at home without prior notice or an outright invitation to do so.

- When entering a Korean home, restaurant, or religious building (such as a temple), it is customary to remove one's shoes.

- Feet are considered unclean and should not touch other people or objects. Men should keep their feet flat on the floor during formal situations.

- When sitting on the floor for a meal, it is customary for men to cross their legs while sitting on the cushion.

- When eating a meal, one should not finish everything on one's plate as it will indicate that one is still hungry.

- In South Korean social settings, good topics of conversation include the Korean cultural heritage, kites, sports, and the health of the other's family (further family inquiries on topics other than health are considered intrusive).

- Topics that should be avoided during social settings include politics, Socialism, Communism, the country of Japan, and the wife of the host.

- When visiting a Korean family, it is appropriate to bring a gift of fruit, imported coffee or quality ginseng tea, chocolates, or crafts from one's homeland.

- When giving or receiving a gift, one should always use both hands. Gifts are not opened in the presence of the giver.

- It is customary to reciprocate a gift with one of similar value and thus, one should choose a gift that takes into account the receiver's economic means.

- After an invitation to dinner at the home of a Korean, one should send a thank-you note to the host.

- Dress in South Korea should be casual and practical outside the office, while suits, for both men and women, are appropriate for most business settings. [28]

---

28   KTNET, Korean Culture (The Trade Automation Service) 1991

TAIWAN – A PART OF CHINA THAT IS NOT PART OF CHINA 6

It's easy while discussing all of this business theory and challenging economic prophesies to forget that, first and foremost, what you'll be doing as you branch out overseas is visiting foreign countries.

Black words on white paper and comforting textbooks perched atop your favorite laptop on the plane ride over are all well and good, but once you step off the neutral territory of that jet, you are, quite literally, in a different world. For instance, during my earliest visits to Taiwan my first impression was one of amazement: Traffic congestion, pollution, loud diners, bikes, scooters, carts and noise, noise, noise.

Even as a seasoned world traveler by that point, Taiwan was like nothing I'd ever experienced before. My first encounter with the traffic in Taiwan was like watching a live version of *Mad* magazine. The closest I can come to visualizing the traffic is that it seems to have no rules. (Actually there are; there is just no enforcement.)

One of the first things my world weary friends advised me about upon hearing I was going to Taiwan was the fact that the pedestrian has NO right of way. None whatsoever. Walking into Taiwanese traffic, you take your life in your own hands. The lack of any visible traffic enforcement whatsoever has caused an amazing, confusing, and extremely intimidating frenzied, continual movement of people, bikes, cars and carts.

I never thought you could put five to six people on a small scooter and successfully drive it in 60 mile-an-hour traffic, and yet this is a common occurrence in Taiwan. People even run across fast moving traffic. When traffic stops for a signal, people don't use cross walks, as they might in your city, they just walk the shortest distance from point A to point B and, more often than not, that could be right between a truck and a car.

I have seen dogs, cats, kids, and businesspeople of all shapes and sizes bump others out of the way and wiggle between gas polluting trucks waiting to sprint from a green light. Cars knocking a pedestrian over were not an uncommon occurrence back in the early 80's.

Thankfully, a lot has changed in Taiwan over the last twenty years. Today, in fact, it's quite a bit different. Don't get me wrong: There is still a lot of traffic, but at least the pollution is a little better and there are less people on a single motorbike (let's say only 2 instead of 5).

What traffic rules that do exist are actually followed a bit better than they were twenty years ago, but you will still be in traffic "shock" when you first observe the congestion and the lack of general rules of the road.

Surprisingly, however, there is very little "road-rage" and most drivers and pedestrians take this maze of congestion for granted. The biggest difference you will observe is the amount of cell phones on the streets. Even by Western/European standards, where cells are quite common, in Taiwan it seems like everyone has one and everyone is talking on one. (Typically, all at the same time.)

However, there are now Starbucks (along with other coffee houses) in Taiwan. It may sounds nuts to even mention it, I know, but not too many years ago it was hard to find ANY coffee, let alone a chain store. Being from Seattle, I know people who TAKE their coffee with them wherever they go. (It's important to remember there are even cultural differences across our own country.)

To a certain extent I would be surprised if you are *not* a bit uncomfortable with all of the confusion I'm describing. Unless you are from India or Los Angeles, you will need a little time to get used to the environment. Thankfully, there are some really nice hotels you can choose from today. Twenty years ago there were only a handful and, at that time, I couldn't afford *any* of them.

Things may have changed a lot for Taiwan, and for you and me, over the last twenty years, but unless we look at history it will be hard to decipher how the Taiwanese live, learn, and prosper. First, a quick geography lesson:

WHERE IS TAIWAN?

I first entered Taiwan during the early 1980's and even at first glance I could see why there had been so many conflicts in its colorful history. A lot of it has to do with its location: Taiwan is a leaf-shaped island about 280 miles long by 60 miles wide. As a frame of reference, it's about 100 miles east of the Fujian province of China. [29]

To the north (about 1,200 miles) is Japan and to the south (just over the horizon) is the Philippine Islands. Unfortunately, Taiwan resides dead center of the typhoon corridor. Of the many days I spent in Taipei, I must say that very few of them were what would be called "nice weather days." Frankly, the weather is generally miserable. Of course, being from the Seattle area, I quickly noticed that the weather is generally the same except for the temperature (which is just this side of blistering) and humidity (just this side of warm soup). Unlike Seattle, however, most people in Taiwan do use umbrellas.

---

29 United States Central Intelligent Agency, The World Fact Book (U.S. Government) 2004

The proximity to Hong Kong (only a few-hour flight) and to other countries makes it highly accessible. So, now that you know where Taiwan is, a little knowledge about its 400 years of history is a requirement before I continue.

The Pre-1600's

The original settlers of Taiwan were people of Malay-Polynesian descent, who initially inhabited the low-lying coastal plains. They called their island Pakan.

During the subsequent settlement by the Dutch and the waves of settlers from China, the aborigines retreated to the hills and mountains, and became known as the "mountain people." Today the remains of about a quarter of a million of these people remain.

The 17th Century

The island's modern history goes back to around 1590, when the first Western ship passed by the island and a Dutch navigator on a Portuguese ship exclaimed, "Ilha Formosa" (meaning "Beautiful island"), which became its name for the next four centuries.

Interestingly enough, the most comprehensive historical records on Taiwan go back some 350 years, to the period of the Dutch occupation, 1624-1662. When the Dutch East Indies Company arrived, they found only the aborigine population on the island: As yet there were no signs of any administrative structure of the Chinese Imperial Government, although there were Imperial expeditions during the 7th and 14th centuries.[30]

Let's pause here for a minute: It is important for the foreigner to remember that both Taiwan and China have conflicting views on the early history of Taiwan. Doing business in both countries gave me an interesting view of their perspective on what happened during these early centuries.

---

30   United States Central Intelligent Agency, The World Fact Book (U.S. Government) 2004

On one hand, China assured me that it was the central power in Taiwan for centuries past. Taiwan, however, argues that China only had a few, brief years of control during the expelling of the Japanese.

And now back to our story: On a narrow peninsula on the Southwestern coast of the island, the Dutch established a fortress named "Zeelandia," after the Dutch province of Zeeland. The peninsula was called Tayouan, meaning Terrace Bay. This later evolved into "Taiwan," and came to be the name for the whole island.

The Dutch brought in Chinese laborers as migrant workers for the burgeoning sugar plantations and rice fields. They usually came for a few years (without family) and then returned to China. Eventually, more settled, and married aboriginal wives. Thus a new race was born: the Taiwanese.

In 1662 the Dutch were defeated by a Chinese pirate, Cheng Cheng-kung (Koxinga), a loyalist of the old Ming dynasty, who himself was on the run from the newly established Ching dynasty. Cheng Cheng-kung himself died shortly afterward, at which point his son took over. But in 1683, this last remnant of the Ming Dynasty was defeated by the Ch'ing troops.

However, the new Manchu emperors were not eager to extend their rule over the island. They were "inland" people with little knowledge of the offshore islands and even less skill at naval warfare.

In the subsequent years, immigration to the island from the coastal provinces of China increased, but the people came mainly to flee the wars and famines on the mainland.

Thus Taiwan remained a loose-lying area for the next 200 years. At times, the Manchu attempted to extend their control over the unruly inhabitants, but time and again the islanders fought back. There were numerous clashes between the local population and officials sent from China, leading to the well-known saying in those days: "Every three years an uprising, every five years a rebellion."

We must, however, remember that trade with China during these times could only occur offshore. Taiwan provided the western traders a great place to port. It was in the middle of the corridor to Japan. Even the Japanese (before they closed their doors to the world) had trading posts on Taiwan. The Spanish were also on the island; that is, until the Dutch kicked them off in 1642.

Even though I consider myself a student of world history by this point, even I am amazed at how many conflicts occurred on this island during these times. There are literally dozens of books written about these times and everyone has a different story to tell. Mine, however, continues:

The 19th Century

It wasn't until 1887 that the Manchu Imperial authorities decided to declare Taiwan to be a "province" of their Empire: They wanted to outmaneuver the Japanese, who were expanding their influence to the south.

The ploy didn't work: In 1895 the Japanese defeated the Manchus in the Sino-Japanese War, and in the Treaty of Shimonoseki, China ceded Taiwan to Japan. The Japanese made a big deal out of this defeat and of obtaining the island "forever."

The Taiwanese didn't like the idea of incorporation into Japan, and on May 25, 1895 – with the assistance of disenchanted Manchu officials – the Taiwan Republic, the first independent republic in Asia, was at last established.

However, a few days later, on May 29, 1895, a Japanese military force of over 12,000 soldiers landed in Northern Taiwan and started to crush the movement. On October 21, 1895 Japanese imperial troops entered Taiwan, the southern capital of the Taiwan Republic, ending its short life.

The Japanese Period

The Japanese occupation might have been harsh, but at least the Japanese were not corrupt. The educational system was built up to the same level as in Japan. Meanwhile, the Taiwanese infrastructures, such as trains, roads, industry etc., were developed extensively. The catch? During these trying times, everything had to be conducted in Japanese.

Why? The Japanese had just opened the doors up to the outside world and wanted Taiwan to be a "showcase" for the rest of the world. The infrastructure that was built during this tumultuous period was a wonderful addition to the country. However, the Taiwanese paid their price as every man and woman literally served the Japanese.

Now, while this was all going on, China had its troubles as well. In 1911, Dr. Sun Yat Shen overthrew the Qing Dynasty and created the Republic of China. For the next 38 years it was a mess of revolts, revolutions, strife, massive corruption, and general misery for the Chinese people.[31]

The next major event that affected Taiwan's status was WW II: During the War, in 1943, the Allied Powers held the Cairo Conference, and on one sleepy afternoon in the hot Cairo sun, they decided to agree with Chiang Kai-shek's request that Taiwan be "returned to (Nationalist) China."

After WWII

When the Japanese surrendered, Taiwan was officially given back to China. For Taiwan, however, it must have been a case of out of the frying pan, into the fire: China, at the time, was a mess.

Chang Kai Shek went on the offense against the Communists. We must remember that Chang was married into one of the (if not the most) wealthiest families in the world (his in-laws were the Soongs and the Kungs). The Chinese people watched as Chang accumulated wealth and Mao scrambled to defeat him.

The tension burst out into the open in the February 28th Incident of 1947, when a small incident in Taipei led to large-scale demonstrations. The Kuomintang was initially taken aback, but secretly sent troops from China, which started to round up and execute a whole generation of leading figures, students, lawyers, and doctors. Between 18,000 and 28,000 people were killed in all, and during the "white terror" of the following years, thousands

---

31   Lai D., A Referendum on Taiwan's Future: No Easy Exit (CSIS Pacific Forum) 2004

of people were arrested, imprisoned, tortured, and murdered by
the KMT's highly efficient KGB-machine, the Taiwan Garrison
Command.[32]

THE BEGINNING OF MARTIAL LAW

In 1949, Chiang Kai-shek lost the war on the mainland, and fled
to Taiwan, where he established the remainder of his regime. For
the next four decades, the people of Taiwan lived under Martial
Law, while the KMT attempted to maintain the fantasy that they
ruled all of China, and would some day "recover" the mainland.
The Chinese mainlanders who came over with Chiang Kai-shek
constituted only 15 percent of the population of the island, but
were able to maintain themselves in a position of power over the
85 percent native Taiwanese through tight control of the political
system, police, military, educational system and media.

What was the interesting event that affected the future business in Taiwan? Well, Chang knew that he must keep the United
States as his ally, for without their protection he was good as dead.
He could not continue to rough up the local people and his own
army was getting restless. He began to develop Taiwan in a way that
would result in a modern miracle that is talked about even today.

Government jobs were created to absorb the military. Schools
were created, as well as roads and a business infrastructure that
allowed people to build their own prosperity. Dissention, however, was not tolerated. The official line of the government was that
Chang was the sole elected government of all of China. Period.

End of story ...

When the Korean and Vietnam War came about, the US supported Chang due to the island proximity to Vietnam and Asia. It
eventually became a military base important to the US. Meanwhile,
Taiwan's economic base began to explode.

---

32 Lai D., A Referendum on Taiwan's Future: No Easy Exit (CSIS Pacific
Forum) 2004

During the following 20 years, from 1952 to 1972, the Kuomintang was able to build up Taiwan economically, thanks to the hard work of the Taiwanese, the sound infrastructure built up by the Japanese, and the need for the US military bases. But on the diplomatic front, they lost ground, and in 1971, their dream world of representing all of China fell apart when Nixon and Kissinger made their "opening" to China.

The diplomatic bomb fell. Basically, Nixon and Kissinger acknowledged that Taiwan was "a part of China" and it was "their problem."[33] The Shanghai Communiqué even implied that U.S. intervention was not to be expected if China attacked Taiwan.

The second diplomatic blow came with Jimmy Carter. Basically, President Carter broke the relationship with Taiwan and established it with China. The US gave up Taiwan for the China connection.

MODERN TAIWAN (AND ME)

By 1980, knowing that they had been isolated diplomatically, Taiwan began what would eventually become their era of "dollar diplomacy." This was a very important economic period for Taiwan. It was also the period when I entered Taiwan.

At the time, the exchange rate was about $38NT for $1USD. At the beginning of the 80's martial law was still in effect, there was no democratic opposition, and it was forbidden to have any contact with mainland China.

Despite these turbulent times, one of my first experiences with an Asian businessperson was actually in Taiwan. I first made contact with Mr. Chen (not his real name) via my trusty Telex machine back in the United States. I found Mr. Chen to be a competent engineer with good values. As a result, I was very much interested in doing business with him and made arrangements to meet with him in Taiwan.

---

33   Shira D., 2004 Business Guide to Shanghai and the Yangtze River Delta (China Briefing Media, Ltd) 2003

During my first visit, I wanted to develop an understanding of his operations and to cultivate our relationship, both business and personal. It was important to develop a mutual trust with Chen, as my potential customers were going to depend on me to provide them a high quality part that was consistent over volume, and Chen was an important ingredient in that particular recipe for success.

If first impressions are, in fact, everything, my first impression with Taiwan didn't bode well: Stepping off the plane I faced my first Typhoon, which promptly blew me back into the old terminal building in Taipei!

I was very familiar with rain, having made my home in the Pacific Northwest, but never had I faced such unmitigated violence in a rainfall, coupled with an amazing amount of humidity. I wasn't sure if my drenched shirt was wet from rain – or sweat. (Neither was very reassuring.) Obviously, not being accustomed to this environment I was an obvious "foreigner" standing on the terminal roadside.

I first met Mr. Chen coming out of the torrent of rain, smiling and extending his hand while welcoming me to Taiwan. (Thankfully, he had an umbrella.) My first impression of Taiwan might have been bleak, but my first impression of Chen was quite the opposite: It was the beginning of a friendship that would last over 20 years. The timing, it seemed, was right: By1986 the push for growth in Taiwan was just at its height.

COTTAGE FACTORIES

Not only was Mr. Chen a much respected design engineer in his own country, but he came equipped with what seemed to me to be an innate sense of "what a foreigner wanted." This was important for me at the time since it was my first step into a different business culture.

Mr. Chen went more than halfway to help my business succeed. By the end of the first day, we shared a lot of ideas about designs and customer needs. We spent most of the day in his small office cluttered with drawings. Stacks of reference books, trade magazines, and various material samples where likewise "organized" on the floor. This only left room for one small chair where I sat wondering what his factory would resemble. The following day we were to drive about an hour outside of Taipei where his "factories" were located.

The next morning, Mr. Chen greeted me with a smile as we began the drive to the rural country. I fully expected a medium size facility, which would greet me with a hum of equipment and the discipline of workers quietly producing quality parts.

I was in for the surprise of my life: The first stop of the day was in a very small village. Parking his car near an open-air market, we began our walk together. Within a few minutes we found ourselves in front of an opened door talking to a young lady with a baby in her arms. After a few introductions, I found myself in her living room.

There, to my amazement, was a piece of equipment where she was apparently "manufacturing" one part of the product I was contracting. She proudly displayed her ability to produce this part quickly and accurately. This was truly an eye opener for me. It was amazing how she could do this with a baby in her arms and another one (they were twins) in a basket, which she rocked with her feet while working.

DEFINITION OF A SMALL BUSINESS...

‹EXCUSE ME A MOMENT, THE RICE IS READY...MEANWHILE, LOOK AT THIS PERFECTLY MADE PART.›

Here I was in a small living room watching production of a part that I was committed to delivering over 10,000 a week with the first delivery in less than thirty days. During the next three hours we walked to 8 different homes. Each home was a different step in the construction of the part. By the last home, the part was complete and packaged carefully into its shipping containers.

At the end of the day, I viewed his full "manufacturing facility" with renewed respect. It actually worked. By the end of the week, I truly believed in Mr. Chen's commitment to the product and to his ability to produce it, on time. I was buying a product from Mr. Chen and it was his word that impressed me.

Over the years, Mr. Chen developed a full factory in Taipei and enjoyed moderate growth. By 1990, he moved his facility to China, thereby tripling his capacity and over the years has enjoyed amazing success. Even today, I buy products from Mr. Chen and he has always upheld his commitments.

I will, however, never forget that first young lady with two babies. Despite my initial shock at not seeing a gleaming factory floor complete with humming machinery and rows of dedicated workers, it was obvious that Mr. Chen treated the people who worked for him with concern and fairness. Mr. Chen's innovation and entrepreneurship was very common in Taiwan at the time. These same people – one might call them pioneers by Taiwan's standards – became their country's modern leaders in innovation and opportunity.

By 1990 the exchange rate was $25NT for $1USD. It was an amazing growth rate for Taiwan and its businesses. The government encouraged factory upgrades and expansions. Marital law no longer existed. There were opposition parties. There was open discussion on the problems with the old party. Contracts were signed with Mainland China. Taiwan began to open up to China and, likewise, China to Taiwan. Taiwan business began to expand into China.

Business was, in a word, booming.

By the year 2000, Taiwan had invested over $30 billion dollars in China. Shipping directly to each other is now available. Direct dial phones are available. This year, direct flights are finally opening. During a recent trip, I was thrilled to see so many talk shows and open street discussions about the island's future and its burgeoning relationship with China.

Opinions about the relationship between Taiwan and China are greatly varied, of course. However, before expressing your own in a business setting, please understand the total situation and the politics of the individual you are talking to. In discussing politics, foreigners (that is you) would do best just to listen and ask polite questions.

That is just one of the social customs I discuss in the following section:

A Few Social Customs in Taiwan

When visiting Taiwan, or any other country, for that matter, remember that you are a visitor in their land, and not the other way around. At all times, respect their social customs and cultural differences. They may seem odd to you but they are a part of their lifestyle and culture and, more importantly, they work for them and can work for you.

Remember my initial shock at seeing that young woman and her two children as they began the process of manufacturing my product? If I had let that visual image detract me from seeing the big picture, the forest for the trees, as it were, I might not have ever done business in Taiwan, let alone done business there for going on three decades.

Particularly, in visiting religious institutions, adhere to a semblance of protocol. Respect their deities. In some cases, you may be required to remove your shoes before you enter a specific area. Observe what others do and, wherever possible, ask if you are not sure. Where questions proliferate, common sense rules.

Here are a few of the most important social customs that you should know:

Your Shoes

In practically every Taiwanese home, as in Japan, guests are requested – you should really read *required* – to remove their shoes even though the host may insist that you don't have to (but that is just a false courtesy). Don't worry about going barefoot, the host always has slippers lying right at the door after you remove your shoes!

The Taiwanese pride themselves in maintaining a clean floor at home. And elsewhere, for that matter: Even in Mr. Chen's cottage factories a guest was required to remove his shoes and put on slippers upon entering. This custom is so important because it displays respect for the homeowner. In the case of the Mr. Chen's cottage factory, I did not take any more than three steps from the door to the equipment. Even in this case, it is very important to remove your shoes, slip on slippers and, only then, step into the home or, in this case, "home factory."

Your Gift Giving

Taiwan (unlike America, I've noticed lately) is a great gift-giving society. When you visit someone's house for dinner, for instance, it is customary to bring a gift. This may be some fruit, a box of chocolates, some pastries, or a bottle of wine. For larger groups or couples one shared gift is acceptable, and maybe some small items for the kids will be enough to score some "brownie points." While most small gifts can be bought in Taiwan, it may be a good idea to bring a few small gifts with you from home to give special friends you will develop.

It must be noted here that the Taiwanese are generally big on brand names and "designer" items, and by this point I always make it a habit to stop by the mall or outlet store before a trip abroad to stock up on such brand-name items that can be bought relatively cheaply in the US but bring serious rewards abroad.

One of my Taiwanese friends was always impressed with items that could only be found as "made in America." Each year it was getting more and more difficult for me to find them before I left for another trip. As more things were being "Made in China" or "Made in Korea," it became a challenge to find that special "Made in America" item for my friend. Finally, after 10 years of gift giving to this person, I could no longer find something "new" that was "made in America."

Upon exclaiming this, he told me, laughingly, that he was "wondering how long it would take me before I ran out of ideas." It seems as though he was playing a joke on me over the course of our decade-long relationship. With the exporting of Taiwan manufacturing he is now bringing *me* gifts.... and now I wonder how long it will be before *he* runs out.

When you present a gift, tradition dictates that it is presented with two hands and received with two hands (the same is true for name cards and anything else exchanged at a social occasion). The host will usually not open the present in your presence, that is, unless you specifically request them to do so. When opening a gift in the host's presence, it is important to open the package carefully to avoid ripping and crumpling the paper. The wrapping paper should be folded up and put aside, not ripped open and promptly disposed of as is usual in other cultures (i.e. the typical American Christmas morning).

For nice presents it is recommended that you wrap it carefully, if not extravagantly, as appearance is important. Don't worry about stocking up back home: There is plenty of wrapping paper available in Taiwan. You can find some, as well as gifts, at Watson's stores or at a bookstore. When giving a gift, it is often customary to demean its value by saying something like, "It's just a small gift to show my appreciation." (Even if it's quite expensive or elaborate.)

Your Omens

Avoid talking about accidents and death; talking about it implies that it might occur. In Chinese, the sound of "four" is similar to death; so hospitals never put patients on the fourth floor and some people do not like to live or have an office on the 4th floor of a building.[34]

It's not easy to escape Asian omens; it seems they creep into everyday life and, more often than not, simple business decisions. Not too long ago I was buying a Sim chip for my cell phone. Buying the Sim chip turned out to be the easiest part; choosing a phone number quickly became an ordeal of sorts.

One of my Taiwanese employees was with me and we stood on the street for half-an-hour looking over the long list of phone numbers that were available. She wanted to make sure that the phone number was a "lucky" one. She even told me that some people would not even dial your number if it were un-lucky.

In Chinese, "white" is associated with death. In giving presents, never use white wrapping paper or white envelopes. Chinese are usually hesitant to leave a will because it indicates the writer is going to die soon. Generally, death is a forbidden topic of discussion.

One of the things I did early in my career was to obtain a Chinese name. What I thought was going to be a fun process, in fact, turned into a very complex and rather serious venture. One of the suggested steps was to hire a fortuneteller that "specialized" in developing lucky Chinese names for the wide-eyed foreigner.

The fortuneteller spent half-a-day with me, following me around and obtaining all sorts of information about me and the history of my family. He then went to work looking at scrolls, charts, and books and spent a lot of time meditating with his deity. Finally, after much pomp and circumstance, he presented my name, which I still hold today.

Regardless of whether you ever take a Chinese name or not, you must take their superstitions seriously and do not "make-fun" or "joke" about their fortunetellers nor their obsession to avoid the "fours."

---

34   C. Bates, Culture Shock! Taiwan (Portland, Oregon, Graphic Arts Center Publishing Company) 2003

Your Guanxi

Shoe-removing and gift-giving are relatively simple concepts to grasp when compared with our next cultural consideration. The word *Guanxi* can be roughly translated as "relationship" or "connections" built up by doing favors for people and having the favors returned. Although it is pretty common in the west, it has become an integral part of social dealings and a sort of unwritten law in the east and thus deserves mention here.

You will need to put some effort into really understanding Guanxi. Relationships and their connections is a basis of how a lot (and I do mean a LOT) of things get done in Taiwan. Knowing that "right" person can mean the difference between getting a factory to run or watching it do nothing. It can mean the difference between becoming a successful businessman in Taiwan or watching others succeed from afar.

I cannot stress the importance of relationships and developing your "bank" of connections throughout Asia. Over the past 20 years, the most important assets I have in Asia are the relationships that I have cultivated.

These relationships, or Guanxi, are based upon the complicated Taiwanese concept known as "face." Actually, Guanxi and Mianzi (saving face) are two different concepts but joined together. The most fundamental cultural difference between Chinese and Americans relates to the role of the individual. The Chinese place great importance on the group consensus and surface harmony.

This is far from a new concept: The issues surrounding "face" have been written about in thousands of books. I have touched on a few critical areas about "face" in this book, but it should really be understood before seriously committing to business dealings in Asia.

That said, I would seriously suggest doing some significant reading about this subject. There are, also, tons of articles and opinions on the web. However, as most of us know, we must be careful about what we read on the Internet, unless it comes from a respected source. I would suggest doing some research at your local university and library to compliment the information you receive from the web. (I have listed some suggested reading at the end of this book to get you started.)

The concept of "face," or "lien" in Chinese, is similar to the western idea of prestige. The opposite being to "lose face" or "dio lien" in Chinese sheds more light on the concept and can be more closely translated to mean "shame." Giving one "word" to another person is a BIG deal. Don't take this lightly.

Face is very important in Eastern cultures, and is especially so in Chinese society. What may simply seem like an obsession with materialism to the western observer is really an integral part of gaining face. Yes, it's a big deal to drive a luxury car. Not that it's just nice on its own, but it's a big part of having good "face."

This particular topic is just a sampling of how we must recognize the differences between our cultures to ensure we are communicating effectively or, at the very least, communicating what it is that we intended in the first place.

I read somewhere (while surfing the web) that a group of Chinese were asked the following: "If you were on a sinking ship with your mother, your wife, and your child and could only save one of them, which one would you save?" Most Americans would quickly respond: "My child, of course." The Chinese, however, responded: "My mother, as I can always remarry and have another child but never could I have another mother." This story is designed to illustrate the differences that can and will occur between two cultures.

I remember a Chinese manager asking a Taiwanese job candidate over a luncheon meeting if he would take personal responsibility for any actions he made on the job. I considered this a very strange question and asked my manager about this after the conclusion of the interview. I always thought that every employee is responsible for his or her own actions (assumed).

Boy, was I wrong: He quickly informed me that the Chinese will not tolerate positions that could hold them to a possible loss of respect should something go wrong. This is very unacceptable to a Chinese person. Therefore, taking personal responsibility opens one up to criticism. For this reason, be very careful how you interview. I am sure that this doesn't hold true to every person in Taiwan, but it illustrates a point one must consider when working across cultures: You can never be too prepared.

Your Business Cards

During your stay in Taiwan, you should always carry your business cards with you. With websites, cell phones, and Email addresses, we here in America have gotten a little lazy about this habit, but it's one you should get back into the swing of when visiting Taiwan. Be forewarned: When you pass them out, you should give them to your business acquaintances with both hands. This is a sign of respect.

Giving business cards is part of the "face" culture. I find that by printing your business cards with English on one side and Chinese on the other, it immediately helps with fostering the future relationship.

Business cards: Don't leave home without them.

Your Invitations

During your stay in Taiwan, you may be invited to a wedding. If you are invited to one, you will be presented with a red envelope, sometimes referred to by foreigners as the "red bomb." The red envelope is not just an "empty gesture," however: You will be expected to bring money when attending the wedding.

Place the money in the red envelope and the typical amount should be about NT$600 to NT$1000 in cash. It may seem crass, but it's actually a pretty fair deal: This entitles you to a wonderful 10-course meal during the wedding party and you are not expected to bring any other gifts. (Hmmm, I wonder if that would work for my daughter's weddings?!?)

PEOPLE WITHOUT A COUNTRY

Catchy title, huh? Well, you might be surprised: This section really isn't about the Chinese, Taiwanese, or even the Koreans. This section is actually about the westerner that refuses to go home once he or she has arrived in China, Taiwan, or Korea.

It is relatively easy to get caught up into a different culture. This especially holds true if one marries into the culture. Once they do, unlike getting married in America, it seems as though they marry every relative and every ancestor their spouse has ever had. One of the first westerners that fit this category was met during my first visit in Taiwan.

Mr. Chen (remember him?) wanted me to have dinner with him and his close friend. I looked forward to meeting them both at his favorite restaurant, which was very close to my (one-star) hotel. Immediately upon arriving for dinner I was introduced to "Jim," who was obviously a westerner. As he vigorously pumped my hand, Jim quickly entered into his story. Did he ever: By the time I sat down at the table I already knew he was born in Southern California, got married, moved to Hawaii, and had seven children.

Turns out Jim and his wife were basically a product of the 60's, or American "flower" children, as they were known. When the Vietnam War broke out, Jim left his wife and fled to Australia, then moved to New Zealand, traveled to Singapore, and finally ended up in Southern Taiwan. By the time he was settling in Taiwan, the war had ended. Jim remarried and began his business in refurbishing Chinese antiques.

Jim's story, although dramatic, is not that unusual for foreigners who remain in foreign countries (whatever their reasons). In today's market, the foreigner who remains in a foreign country (otherwise known as an expatriate, or "Expat" for short) is managing their time between the home country and the foreign location. They are usually professional businessmen or women who understand the needs for cross cultural considerations and they make sure they return to the "home country" on a managed schedule.

There are many stories similar to Jim's. For that reason, it is important for the international manger to manage their Expats carefully and become more involved with the country of choice. (Rest assured, I go into this consideration further in my upcoming chapter on Expats.)

Back to our story about Jim: The last time I heard about Jim was in the late 1980's. He was caught trying to take some antiques out of China and the last sight of Jim was running down the side-walks in Guangzhou with the authorities behind him. The moral of the story is to respect the country you are in, and abide by their laws. It's their country and their rules. Therefore, learn them and abide by them. (Or wind up like Jim!)

NOT UNDERSTANDING BUSINESS METHODS

During the early 1990's I was looking for a manufacturer of bags. This was a bit out of my expertise at the time, as my specialty during those days was primarily electronic components. However, one of my customers who manufactured a portable instrument wanted to offer a carrying bag to their customers, so I quickly made it my business.

My client wanted to outsource the production of this bag as, at that time, about 30% of their sales were in Taiwan and that was also where the majority of the requests for the "hand-bags" were coming from. Therefore, to eliminate shipping costs, they were carefully considering contracting with manufactures in Taiwan. I had been supplying components to them for close to 10 years by this point and was asked to look into this possibility.

This was not an unusual case for my company. There have been many times when I would help our customers with these types of requests, even though they were, as I said, not exactly "my bag."

Through several long days of hard work, research, and quite a bit of shoe leather, the selection of the manufacturer was at last between two different companies. One of them was in Southern Taiwan. Fortunately, I had previously visited this company a few times and was beginning to get to know Mr. Chou, the General Manager, quite well. He and his wife had entertained me a few times and were even comfortable enough to invite me to their home. I found that Mr. Chou was a very honorable person who kept his word, even to the point of losing profit.

During my visit concerning the bag matter, I noticed that he was very stressed over some small handbags he had manufactured earlier. During my inquiry into the matter, his story began: It seems as though he had started establishing a business relationship with a distributor of bags in Australia. After months of faxes and phone calls, the president of the company visited him personally.

The young lady, we'll call her "Sally" here, arrived at the appointed time with orders in hand and began negotiating payment terms almost immediately. This made Mr. Chou fairly uncomfortable, as he wanted some time to enjoy the tea his assistant had prepared and develop a relationship with this potential client. Sally was interested in neither tea nor conversation, but instead wanted to know if Mr. Chou would accept 60-day terms. This all occurred within the first hour of Sally's arrival at the factory.

Mr. Chou knew that the potential for his factory was very large. In fact, if he believed in Sally's estimated quantities for production, it would double his output. Mr. Chou wavered, but finally agreed to Sally's aggressive terms. Even though the initial orders were very small in comparison with Sally's estimated annual quantities, he wanted to support the relationship and develop a long lasting business friendship. Boy, was he in for a surprise.

Mr. Chou, knowing Sally's estimated annual quantity, ordered raw material that could support six months of these quantity estimates. This allowed Mr. Chou to buy the bulk material at a price point that would allow him to break even on the smaller, start up quantity he was currently producing and, later, eventually profit when Sally's orders reached her projected annual estimate.

Mr. Chou's supplier was a long time friend of Mr. Chou's and their business was based on Guanxi and Mianzi, or the complicated Taiwanese concept of winning or losing "face." It was a bit of a legacy, I suppose: Their fathers were doing business with each other long before them. Mr. Chou was giving 75-day terms on this order to support the aggressive business style of Sally.

Sixty days after his shipment to Sally, Mr. Chou received a short fax. Sally briefly stated that she wanted another 30 days before she would be able to pay Mr. Chou's invoice. Mr. Chou was, in a word, crushed.

This is when I happened to arrive. Mr. Chou told me the story and he couldn't understand how anyone could change their request after giving (what he thought) was their mutual "word" on the arrangement. Obviously, Sally was still working in her own cultural understanding and had no idea of the concept of doing business in Taiwan or, for that matter, "saving face."

It certainly doesn't make Sally a bad person; just a bad judge of character. In our own country, for instance, we tend to see terms as a flexible item, fair to negotiate depending on cash flow. Even my own bank has given me advice on how to "manage" our Accounts Payable department by "stretching" out the suppliers, thereby giving us better "cash management."

Be careful, however, as this can be a very costly decision when faced with a Taiwanese business proposition. Even *asking* to do something like this can cause loss of face and a drastic loss of business.

In the case of Sally, she never took the time to really understand Guanzi or Mianzi. This was a fatal mistake. Mr. Chou could not renegotiate with his suppliers, as that would be a loss of "face" and, frankly, unthinkable to him. Mr. Chou's perception of Sally was that she lost her "face" and dishonored herself; therefore he could no longer trust her with ANY business. He decided to stop all production, return what merchandise he had produced, and write off the finished goods at a loss.

For her part, Sally was confused and felt Mr. Chou broke their contract.

Lesson learned? What we consider a "normal" business practice in the United States may not actually be the case in the foreign country. You must do your homework BEFORE you start negotiating. BEFORE you start conducting "normal" management practices, ask yourself if this is the appropriate behavior in the other culture.

If it's not, or if it's even questionable, go back to the drawing board and come up with an offer that might make both parties happy, given the country's particular cultural considerations.

Sometimes giving our "word" in our own culture is only marked by intent. In Mr. Chou's culture, however, it's a binding statement that cannot be broken. In fact, in the case of Mr. Chou, I have learned over the years that he would literally sacrifice his own salary, profit, etc. to keep his word. Sally just looked at the "agreement" and sent a fax off to see if he would support her situation, which was not foreseen at the time of the original negotiation. It might have seemed an innocent oversight at the time, in retrospect, but it soon became deadly as she really didn't consider the cultural differences.

What happened with my handbag offer? Fortunately, I saw the opportunity to obtain material at a discount and committed to Mr. Chou our small contract to purchase the material he committed from his friend. This simple solution actually had two major benefits: First, it allowed Mr. Chou to "save face" and, secondly, it raised my relationship "status" with Mr. Chou.

By the way, unlike Sally, I always pay my committed invoices early. Before you give your "word," make sure you REALLY KNOW WHAT IT MEANS.

Chinese culture is based upon shame. This means that the individual will pursue what is considered the "proper" action UNLESS "scorn" is brought upon oneself or the family (or even his or her social group).

CROSS CULTURAL CONSIDERATIONS WITH THE TAIWANESE

During the 1990's there was a transformation in process throughout Taiwan. Most manufacturing companies were moving across borders to find lower cost operations. It is interesting to note here that this is not as unusual as you might first think. Consider your own country and notice a movement toward global integration.

In Taiwan, it occurred quickly and to the most obvious country: China.

I asked one of my suppliers, Mr. Chen, why this was occurring. He replied that, "It's relatively easy as we speak the same language and have the same culture. It's like going home to visit your distant relatives."

What happened (and what is still continuing to this day) is that the Taiwanese are going "global" at a rate that is much faster than most other countries. This is occurring for many reasons, but I find one of them very interesting: One of my Taiwanese friends explained that the Taiwan business market has always been international. Most of their products are exported and over the years they have developed a good sense of international marketing. They didn't just start in the 90s; they've actually been doing it for some time.

When I set up my first factory in Southern China, a large number of my business relationships were with Taiwanese who were already in China manufacturing their product. It was like thinking that you were really the first to be climbing a particular mountain only to find out that someone has already beat you to it. In fact, they not only beat you to it but have also built a resort at the top!

During my visit to Vietnam (see the Chapter on Vietnam) I not only met with Japanese businessmen but with a large group of Taiwanese businessmen who have been manufacturing in Southern Vietnam for years prior.

Historically, Taiwan was looked upon as a fun, freewheeling place where it was great to do business. It is still a bit like that today, but they have taken what they have learned over previous decades and are now applying it in other countries all over the world.

The important lesson to learn with this chapter is that wherever you go to set up a factory in the world, it would not surprise me that you will discover a Taiwanese that has already been there before you. Because of this, you must understand their culture to effectively work with them. I know of a Taiwanese businessman doing business inside of Russia! While in Russia, therefore, we need to have an understanding of both Russian and Taiwanese cultural differences in order for us to be effective businessmen.

A Few Words of Caution

(From Personal Experience)

As always, I reserve judgment about the countries, or the people in those countries, where you might one day do business. It is important to know, however, that in China I have seen the Chinese not look upon the Taiwan manager with much grace (and for good reasons).

I'll share with you a personal anecdote to explain why: Two Taiwanese businessmen operated one of my factories. Both of them had years of experience with operating a factory inside of China and became key personnel in the setup and initial operations of the new factory. What I didn't know until months later, however, was that they were taking advantage of the employees.

Our factory produced a certain amount of waste (non-polluting) that we sold each month to a recycling facility. One of the programs we set up was to take this money and put it away in a bank. It was only to be used for employee care. For example, if an employee needed special care or items that would improve their well-being (i.e. shoes, clothes, etc.) the money would be allotted to them from this special bank account we had set up. It was a great idea that, unfortunately, went nowhere.

About one year into this program I found out that the scraps were, in fact, being sold but the money never arrived at the bank. The person in charge of the program was diverting the funds to his or her own pocket and not telling anyone. It turned out that it was one of the Taiwanese managers. The comments that were generated by my Chinese staff were, surprisingly, not of anger or even disgust. It was, as one of them stated, "Expected."

I have found that there is distrust (some of it founded on fact) between the Chinese employee and the Taiwanese manager. There is, also, some tension between the reverse. Remember: Not all things are what they seem.

I am certainly not claiming this will occur in all cases, but the thing to remember here is that when you mix multinationals together you, as their manager, have a different set of issues you must manage. It no longer follows the old rule of managing people from the same culture. The differences are, sometimes, deeply rooted in political and old social methods that are based in ancient belief systems. This, coupled with some personal prejudices, can lead to very difficult management issues.

Being aware of these differences will allow you to prevent some disaster in the short and long term. There is an old saying that my Grandmother used to repeat: "An ounce of prevention is worth a pound of gold." So, do your homework before you start mixing cultures. (And save yourself that pot of gold.)

THE FUTURE

As we can certainly see from this chapter and others, the transition of high-technology manufacturing industries to China is certainly the ongoing trend that will likely continue for years to come.

With the benefits of low-cost outsourcing versus the cost of maintaining a higher cost of manufacturing on the island, there is a strong possibility that the Taiwanese industries will just be a series of expatriate corporations. These corporations may be legally based in Taiwan, but in reality will become an integral part of Mainland China's economy. Taiwan is entering an era during which their economy will closely resemble a shell of corporate HQ locations with the bulk of their operations scattered over Asia.

Under this assumption we can foresee a couple of scenarios for the global businessperson. The first is that the Chinese could nationalize Taiwanese industrial factories located in China. Simply put, they could just take them over and tell the world that they "belong to China." This would seem to some people a prelude to declaring war on each other, but the recently avowed relationship with the United States provides a hedge against this kind of aggression. Besides, owning a factory is one issue but a bigger issue is to operate and market its *product*. I have seen Chinese government facilities being converted to commercial industries. It is difficult and it's a slow evolution.

The second outcome is more mutually beneficial: China and Taiwan could become more increasingly interconnected in their dealings and relationships. The eventual reunification of Taiwan and China under peaceful terms is, I believe, a likely outcome. Of course, it remains to be seen what transition will actually be taken.

The key to the future of this relationship is the positive transition of information technology between the two countries. If this occurs and the two develop a successful interconnect, the effects on both nations would be an important turning point in their economy.

Now, how about you and I?

Taiwan is certainly a country of entrepreneurs. Their cultural belief system drives them to be their own bosses. Obviously, not all Taiwanese do this (no large corporation would exist) but there is a trait that is unique to the Taiwanese that is rooted in the entrepreneurial spirit. This continues to this day.

A few of my hard won lessons along the way when working with Taiwanese have taught me to really understand their cultural belief systems before putting them in a critical position of managing people of other cultures.

The other thing that you should be aware that does exist to the Taiwanese (and the Chinese) is nepotism. Basically, they don't trust anyone outside their own family unit. These are strong words but they need to make an impact on the prospective manager. I find company after company who has a multiple of family members working for the "father."

If you are hiring for or own a company in Taiwan, I would seriously consider banning the practice of hiring any relatives. This is a preventative measure that will reduce the belief that the family's interest comes before the company's. Trust me, hiring a relative leads way to some shady things (been there....seen this). Typically, this runs from a dual set of books to skimming money for the "brother's education." If you are looking into purchasing a company or setting up a joint venture, be very careful.

I would just make it a predominate rule not to hire relatives and to eliminate inter-office dating (just make it a policy: if you date, one of you has to go). Remember Grandma's prevention statement, and the fact that despite being culturally aware, it doesn't mean you have to be culturally subservient. You are still the customer, you are still the boss. Tread that fine line between being culturally considerate, but don't tow it to the exclusion of common sense.

PARTING WORDS

There is a predominate question that always arises from my customers and startup entrepreneurs, which is always the same: "How do I get started?"

With the Chinese based cultures it is critical that you establish your "network." This is a big buzzword in the US, but trust me it becomes even more important in Asia. Without the right "network" of people you will have trouble even getting out of the starting gate, let alone becoming successful.

Take a cue from Asian customs: One of the areas to start with is your own family. Do they have any connections? If they don't have any contacts within your country of choice, then you are faced with making them on your own. It may be a difficult challenge, but make them you must.

I cannot stress enough the importance of making contacts. Once you get the first contact, it can (and should) help generate the next two. Once you make one contact, then ask for the next two you should call (and ask for a reference; get them to call ahead for an introduction). By doing this each time, your network will grow quickly.

Depending on what you want to accomplish, this will define the type of contact you will need. Some of the places to start (besides your family members, that is) are your attorney, other businessmen, the US Commerce Department, your local World Trade Center, your home state trade organizations, and the Internet (try emailing a few people, you will be surprised at the responses you get back).

Make sure you keep up with maintaining your contacts. That means writing thank you notes, making follow-up calls, accepting – or offering – invitations to dinner, going to play golf with them, etc. Managing your contact list means giving up some of your office time to develop the relationships that will ensure profits and success. Whatever you do, remember my comments on relationships: They are THE most important element in being successful in Asia.

There are thousands of books available to the prospective global entrepreneur to help with these issues. But you don't have to hunt them all down for yourself, as I have listed a few of my favorites at the end of this book.

In summary, Taiwan is a very important country to understand and, to understand the Taiwanese, you must develop an appreciation for their culture. Your network of people should include someone from the Taiwan business community. Even if you are trying to do business in Vietnam, you will certainly be facing a Taiwanese business associate that will already be there.

THE EXPAT – A HIGH-RISK EMPLOYEE FOR THE GLOBAL ENTREPRENEUR 7

TO EXPAT OR NOT TO EXPAT:

That is Really the Question

Starting, or expanding, a company overseas is an inherently risky proposition. Please don't let my confidence in foreign markets or glowing reports of foreign dignitaries blind you to the fact that doing business overseas is still doing business.

And, as with all businesses, there are risks involved. As the recent tsunamis in Indonesia and Thailand reveal, nothing is a sure thing and Mother Nature, not to mention foreign governments, have a way of being unpredictably unpleasant.

But sometimes it's neither nature nor the government in these foreign trade zones that poses the greatest risk, but indeed the people you hire to make, sell, or distribute whatever product your company manufactures.

If you've never heard the term expatriate before, though they're most commonly referred to as "Expats," then there's never been a better time to start. First, let's first define an "Expat." From the dictionary we find the following definition:

---

ex·pa·tri·ate

v. ex·pa·tri·at·ed, ex·pa·tri·at·ing, ex·pa·tri·ates

> *v. tr:* To remove (oneself) from residence in one's native land.

> *n:* voluntarily absent from home or country

ex·pat

> *n.* Chiefly British; Ex-Patriate (see above)

Now, don't get me wrong: I'm not condemning all Expats. In my opinion, frankly, there is a difference between an Expat and someone who is on an international assignment or task.

For the purpose of this particular chapter, an assignment will be defined as "…someone sent to a foreign country with a length of term usually less than 6 months but never more than 12 months."

In other words, it's temporary …

And therein lies the difference: A person on an international assignment does not necessary relocate to the foreign office but the tenure could be as short as a few days to as long as 6 months. An Expat, on the other hand, relocates his living artifacts to the foreign country for a longer tenure. An Expat, therefore, gives up his residence in favor of the foreign country. Basically, they "live" in the foreign country for an extended length of time (over 6 months).

What do I know about Expats? Plenty, trust me, but my first introduction came about as will many of yours: Necessity is the mother of all invention. Or, in this case, discovery: During the mid-90s my company's growth was expanding at a rate that made it quite clear that if we were going to succeed, we needed a different management team.

It also became apparent that we needed to expand our facilities in China and develop our own manufacturing enterprise. Naturally, I couldn't do everything myself and couldn't be everywhere at the same time. (Although during those formative years it often felt like I was being pulled in two different directions, or at least meeting myself coming and going!)

To resolve these issues of delegation and micro-management, it soon became clear to me that what I really needed was an individual who could live in China and oversee the new factory *for* me.

This was an exciting time, but one that deserved a hefty dose of caution. I was not sure who to trust and knew without a doubt that the person who I hired for this position would need to be trusted without fail. Thus I began researching for ways to solve this particular problem and eventually discovered the "Expat." I thought my troubles were over, only to find out later that they were, in fact, only starting.

I was relieved to discover that there is a wealth of information out there on the subject of Expats, and most of it's at your fingertips. Books, magazine articles, the Internet, it's all out there waiting to be gathered, collected, devoured.

Unfortunately, 99% of it is devoted to the *romance* of being an Expat and the inherent exploitation of all the perks that come with the job. It was an eye-opening experience for a potential employer to read all of these books and articles out there written about how to *exploit* an employer. From what I could garner, there is a basic view that companies wishing to employ an Expat must pay everything.

And I do mean *everything*. Housing, food, children's private education, spouse's car and driver, recreation, travel cost to see relatives, to mention just a few. Actually, as an employer, we directly pay for all this anyway. It's called the salary we give to the employee. However, with an Expat it's all additional pay…. and pay…. and pay…. and pay.

Before we get into these specifics of working with an Expat, let's try to save you the time and money by first figuring out if we even need one of your employees to go to your foreign factories in the first place:

The Need for Speed

By the time you find yourself struggling to determine the psychology of the Expat you should have already determined a need for someone to help you manage, or bridge, a cultural canyon. If you haven't, then go back to the drawing board and start figuring out if you REALLY need someone.

Let's consider, first, where you might find yourself tempted to make such a decision as hiring an Expat. After all, why take the aspirin if you don't have the headache, right? Here are some of the reasons that other companies use Expats (as strange as it sounds).

1. Cannot figure out how to get rid of that older employee? Simply make him an Expat:
   a. Strange as this sounds, a number of larger companies use the Expat position to "put the old guy out to pasture." In some cases (although rarely, in my experience) it actually works!
   b. How to *reward* the old guy? Send him to one of your nicer locations.
   c. Want to get rid of the mediocre employee? Send him to the *worst* location.

2. That competitor is driving you nuts in the foreign country? Make your sales manager an Expat.

3. Don't want to travel? Cannot cope with cultural diversity? Hire an Expat.

This list can go on, as one might imagine from the variety of reasons we've just explored, but you get the basic idea. For that reason, there are a lot of Expats out there for the wrong reason. To avoid making the same mistake yourself, let's remember a few things: 1.) it can be VERY expensive to send someone overseas AND 2.) most companies *don't* get their return on the investment.

This isn't just my opinion; it's a fact that there are more failures than successes when it comes to an Expat. In fact, here was a study done by some very serious researchers, as published in the March-April 1999 issue of *Harvard-Business Review*, who accumulated some interesting data from calling on companies and talking to the CEO's and H.R. Managers for over 10 years.

Here is a brief summary of some of their findings:

1. Between 10 and 20 percent of all managers sent abroad returned early due to dissatisfaction or difficulties with the job. (In other words, "I quit.")

2. Of those who stayed over 30% did not perform to the satisfaction of the company. (In other words, "I'm fired.")

3. Another 25% left the company and joined a competitor. (In other words, "I'm educated now and I want *your* customers.")

If running a business overseas is an inherently risky proposition, then hiring an Expat to run your overseas business *for* you is a doubly dicey call. You simply cannot assume that the rules for management (the ones that appear to work, anyway) in your own country work the same in every country. Frankly, they don't.

Worse yet, they often work to a counter effect. In fact, you can take your own countrymen and put them in your factory (but in a different country) and you have a good chance that he will be working for a competitor in a few years and going after your old customers.

Even though the picture I paint does not tend to encourage anyone to hire an Expat consider, if you will, a sobering statement from the same article:

"In today's global economy, having a workforce that is fluent in the ways of the world isn't a luxury, it's a competitive necessity. Nearly 80% of midsize to large companies currently employee Expat's and 45% of them are going to INCREASE the number they have abroad."

In order to be competitive, therefore, you must think global. Their data was taken and compiled by 1998-1999. I would expect that the 80% they mentioned is already outdated and, in fact, had risen to the mid-90% by 2004.

After talking to a number of small companies I find that they are re-writing their business plans to incorporate global marketing (including how to compete with similar companies halfway around the world). This means that even small businesspeople who only have one or two employees are already developing global plans. Welcome to the 21st Century of business. If you are not actively thinking global, it is clear that you will lose market share, lose profitability, and lose cost controls if you don't start soon.

For now, let's get back to the Expat question. (Or, as I like to call it, the "Expat equation.") Expats are usually hired for the wrong reasons, or reasons that are obviously unfounded. Here is a case in point:

Delegating Down Under

A few years ago I spent a couple of days in Hong Kong at the end of a long trip in China to wind down and reflect on its results. I often find that by taking a day or two off at the end of my trip I can summarize my notes and devise better planning tactics for the next trip. When traveling abroad, creature comforts, or at least the illusion of them, can become increasingly important. During those days I would always stay at the same hotel as it gave me a sense of "home."

The hotel bar was small and intimate and occasionally even allowed me some quiet time to gather my thoughts. During one such time I bumped into an Australian businessman who, like me, was simply searching for the creature comforts of home.

Slumped over his evening drink, he seemed a bit distant and apparently stressed. As he was the only other person in the bar, I asked if he would like some company for a few minutes. He hesitantly agreed. During our subsequent discussion I began listening to his story about the company he worked for in Sydney.

As the VP of Operations of a medium sized textile firm his directive (given about five years prior) was to establish manufacturing facilities in China. Within the first three years he established three factories, each one doing a different product series for world distribution. At the end of five years, the CEO was very upset with the financial condition of the China operations. It was continuously losing money by an excess of 1 million dollars (US Dollar equivalent).

Each plant was operated by a hand-selected Australian Expat with a minimum of 10 years experience within the company. The CEO was apparently adamant about his own countryman running his plants. They concluded that they wanted to ensure that their company's culture was transferred quickly to the factories. Despite their losses, the management staff was sure that if they placed a Chinese manager in charge they would lose communication ability and, as a result, control. In addition, the CEO did not have any confidence in Chinese managers.

Even though the CEO had never been outside of Australia.

The V.P., let's call him "Sam," continued his story and, as he warmed to the subject, the drinking of his beer began in earnest. It seemed as though each factory was "managed" by an Expat. Furthermore, he estimated that each Expat cost the company (including benefits) an average of $560,000.00 each.

The company paid for their children's education, the spouse, their home, food allowance, travel expenses and three months of vacation pay per year. (Think *that's* bad? A few years later I was talking to a CEO who has an Expat in Saudi Arabia. He estimated it cost his company in excess of $4 million US Dollars for one Expat over a three-year period!)

Sam began explaining that he wanted to hire Chinese managers shortly after each factory became operational. He and his staff calculated that by having him visiting on the same frequency as his present schedule it would ensure the company would stay on-track with production and quality. This solution would save the company in excess of 1.3 million per year, thereby reversing the financial picture and putting it in a profit mode.

Unfortunately, Sam's CEO and the Board of Directors discarded Sam's suggestion and proceeded with the Expat formula. Jumping ahead five years, Sam suddenly finds himself telling me the conclusion of his sad story: His recent trip just concluded him shutting down all three factories.

The ripple effect of such a decision can be enormous, and not just for the parent company. For instance, this particular action put over 2,000 Chinese employees out of work. It also obligated his company to repatriate the Australians and move them back to Australia with an estimated cost of $150,000 per family. It furthermore reduced their global sales by 13 million dollars and severely damaged their public relations image. In fact, the PR department was now a vacant room as they all left to the competitor, who was actively gobbling up their global market share in the huge vacuum left by the closed factories. A publicly traded company, the stock dropped 18% within a week after announcing the plant closures.

Naturally, Sam's job was now at risk.

Though empathetic with Sam's situation, I was naturally aghast by how anyone could isolate him- or herself for so long with such an apparently gigantic problem. Sam explained that the company's H.R. Department never worked abroad and other than himself (and the three Expats) no one in the company had ever worked in another country.

It was apparent that the CEO and his staff had little understanding as to the unique challenges that lay ahead with this global assignment. Nor did they consider either personal or professional challenges on the bumpy road ahead.

In Sam's case, they got bogged down in middle management administration and CEO fears instead of capturing strategic opportunities. There was no global leadership development, they had no cross-cultural abilities, and they overextended themselves with Expats.

No doubt it had been a good idea for this company to consider manufacturing in China. This gave them an extended market (they sold their product in China, Korea, Hong Kong and Vietnam) and assured greater profitability (by meeting the price point necessary to extend their market). However, they did not follow through to ensure good cost management. By not developing Chinese managers to oversee the native work force, it essentially blinded the company to other options: "I must use Expats to ensure corporate culture." Poor global management led them to critically damaging their company.

Don't get me wrong: Initial setup using a "team" from corporate headquarters is very sensible. However, using Expats extensively is dangerous and usually leads a company right down the road to failure. It's a case of sending the right people for the wrong kind of reasons, a scenario that, unfortunately for many companies, is doomed to failure.

In the case of Sam's company sending an Expat, it was initially a good idea. It ensures that the manufacturing processes and set-up meets the quality standard of the parent company. Where most companies fail, however, is that they stop there. To keep the positive momentum going and make the overseas transition an effective and smooth one that Expat, or the "team" that accompanied him or her, should be expected to transfer this knowledge to the local professional. Once these vital steps are accomplished then it is important to get the Expat out of the country.

Fast!

It's amazing to see the Expat industry at work. You can go to the Internet and find a ton of information related to the Expat. You can even go to Amazon.com and find books not only about being an Expat, but books written by Expats themselves. I've read some. You know what the authors talk about? They basically say how great the profession is and how successful they are.

Wow, wonder where they get *that* personal statistic?

Of course, for the manager considering all of this, it's the mistakes made by other companies that need to be learned. Observing other people's mistakes is critical. Through such test cases we ourselves can learn *not* to make them. Now, I am assuming that the reader is not working for a company like Nokia. After all, they use international assignments just to gain knowledge for the individual. (Nice luxury.) In the real world, of course, most small business people don't have the resources of a company like Nokia. However, we can – and should – still learn from them.

Now, I am going to assume that you are not trying to use an overseas assignment to become a global political leader, global teacher nor just to gain knowledge for the fun of it. Also, you must consider that an international assignment must (MUST) go beyond the immediate assignment.

To put it bluntly, an Expat should *only* be used for a few months at the most UNLESS there is a defined, written goal and you are willing to pay hundreds of thousands of dollars to achieve that goal. If not, forget the Expat. In my opinion, and the opinion of dozens of well-respected CEO's, they are overrated and very much overpaid for the new generation of global businesses that is arising in the 21st Century business world. Any profession that only has an 11% success rate, I naturally question using them.

I should clarify that I do profess to use an Expat, but only when it really makes sense. Not that I haven't made mistakes with Expats. (Wow, have I ever!) The biggest danger of having an Expat for long-term employment is that they morph into something you might never expect. (I call these the Hybrid and King Effects, respectively.) To assess the dangers of either, let's first look at both:

THE HYBRID EFFECT

Basically, the longer an Expat is overseas the more they become what I call a "hybrid of cultures." I have read books that profess to using the three-year rule with Expats. They state: Never, but never, leave a person overseas more than three years. If you do, they become a person without a country (without a culture is more applicable). Personally, I could cut a year off of that philosophy. I believe this effect begins to surface in about the 24th month. This depends on the individual, of course, but nonetheless this effect *will* happen.

It's just a matter of time.

The most obvious (and extreme) symptom is the 50-year-old Expat marrying a 21-year-old woman from a different culture. Silly as it seems, I have seen this happen quite a few times. Cultural differences can seem very romantic and the cultural characteristics of behaviors between sexes can be huge. An evening foot massage to one culture shows a sign of respect and reverence. To another, it's subservience and submission. Therefore, if your employee is ignorant about the other culture, they may assume the action as something different than the intent.

Trouble often follows …

Other effects that can be noticed are the dependence on various services. This includes the "I cannot do anything without my car and driver" or "I am not sure if I can go without having my cook less than 5 days a week." (As you might imagine, other names for the Hybrid Effect include the Movie Star Effect and the Ambassador Effect!)

Whatever you call them, these are sure indicators of the beginnings of the inevitable transformation of the Expat. However, the *real* problem comes when you want the Expat back at corporate headquarters and is transferred. Then the problems really start. As we saw in the Harvard article, this is where lots of people quit and move on or are simply fired. All of a sudden they have to wash their own clothes or drive the car themselves.

The nerve!

This is the reason why time is of the essence: To reduce this particularly unpleasant effect the Expat must be "cycled" and not be left on his own for any length of time. I would suggest a 12-18 month maximum cycle. If you leave them beyond this amount then re-training will be a mess and repatriation becomes almost an impossibility. Check out your H.R. Department. If there is no one there who has been on an international assignment, you're in trouble (or should I say the Expat is in trouble).

This effect is slow moving. It's going to have an effect on the Expat; it's just a matter of time. Therefore, the length of time during which he is left alone is critical. The length depends on the Expat, you, and the support your company gives to your team. Training is critical; authority is vital.

It is important that long-term programs are discussed and designed *before* you consider sending anyone on an international assignment. This includes you, if you are going overseas for any length of time.

Remember: The Hybrid Effect works on CEOs, too!

THE KING EFFECT

If the Hybrid Effect holds great potential for abuse, then the King Effect is sure to cause trouble. Much like an abusive king, it quietly spreads and then quickly becomes too late for the company to easily solve. Thanks to the law of cause and effect, the King Effect usually begins only after the Hybrid Effect is too long ignored. As you might expect, I have had personal experience with this unfortunate effect:

A few years before I set up a manufacturing facility, I was introduced to a British businessman (lets call him "James") who recently completed a factory closure in China (he sold it to the employees). He knew I was working out a plan to open a component manufacturing facility in Southern China and he shared some of his experience with me. It was wonderful to hear his story and it gave me some insight in regard to working with Expats.

His story revolved around managing his new Expat employee. James knew this person (let's call him "George") for 15 years before he hired him. He became a business friend and he had offshore experience with other companies (traveling abroad to inspect factories and negotiate contracts). They used to travel together and share notes and ideas about certain facilities and people they'd encountered therein. George's most acclaimed success was that he had set up a manufacturing facility and became profitable within three years. Within five years George was reassigned to China to develop relationships for the facility in his home country.

George, being in his late forties, did not have the greatest marriage at the time. As their children were grown up and out on their own, this gave George and his wife, Sally, time to reflect on their own personal relationship. (As I am not a mystery writer, I am sure we all know where *this* story is going.)

George had a history of separation from his wife. On a few occasions, in fact, he left only to return "for the sake of the children." Now, we weren't gossiping for gossip's sake: James was merely stating a few personal items about George to make a point: You must REALLY know the personal aspects of a prospective Expat to make a good decision on his or her stability. I know that there are laws that restrict our looking into certain aspects of an individual's life, but it's critical to know as much about the person SOCIALLY as possible. At its core, this tragic story is a simple one of obvious mismatching.

If you are placing a person in a cross-cultural situation, then you need to know his/her stability in their present culture. You need to start looking in their closets. Not for suits or ties, but any skeletons that might reside therein.

Let's continue with James' story about George: George's last assignment found him stationed in China, alone, trying to assist his company to expand into different markets. The company was experiencing annual sales of an excess of 100 million per year and was looking for the "right opportunity."

George's boss just happened to be the founder and owner of the company. Well into his 70's at this point, he was concerned about the "non-Christian views of the Chinese" and had reservations using any of them as primary managers. Being a fellow countryman, George provided the CEO with the comfort level he required.

As with most economies the market quickly took a turn for the worse and found this company losing 30% of their sales within a few short months. Not everyone in the company was suffering as a result: By this time George was separated from his wife and was on the prowl in China to find a "relationship" that matched his desires. About the time his interviewing was completed and his "find" was comfortably living with him, his company closed the doors on China and asked him to return.

George wasn't about to move; he liked his evening foot massage.

During this time James was seriously looking into setting up his own manufacturing inside of China. James's company profitability was slowly shrinking, margins were reduced to keep their customers, and overhead cost was reduced to a minimum. James needed to bypass contract manufacturing and help his company produce their own products themselves.

George's technical ability was what was needed. Unfortunately, James didn't take a longer-term look at George's cultural and business ability. All due respect for George, James wasn't a good global manager at this time. Between the two of them, it was a sure road to long-term failure.

Let's discuss the situation at this point in time to find any foreshadowing of future problems: One of the primary reasons for sending anyone overseas MUST go beyond the immediate problem. Foreshadowing? Two immediately spring to mind: James was focused on the necessity of immediate profit. George was focused on the immediate need to stay in China.

The first two years were devoted to George learning about their products and setting up the initial process. It took twice as long and twice the amount of money. Listening to legal advice (remember, this was in the 90's) James set up a separate company in Hong Kong and used this entity as the holding company for the Chinese operations (both a representative office and a factory).

George hired a long time friend, a Taiwanese (I will call him "Pete"). Pete was an experienced salesman and sold extensively throughout China to other foreign companies (primarily the Japanese and Taiwanese). George placed Pete in the coveted position of factory manager. Likewise, both George and Pete owned minority shares in the Hong Kong company.

George very seldom went to the factory. He stated that it was "Pete's operation" and he "ran the show." In response, Pete hired other Taiwanese to manage the Chinese workers. The company operations grew and doubled its size in the third and fourth years. They reached profitability during the fourth year. James had invested over $750,000 to reach this stage.

James knew that to begin global expansion he needed to begin integrating the British operations with the China operations. The separation of the two was quickly becoming an issue as each company wanted to profit from the same customer. James wanted to bring these two management groups together and devise a single business plan for both companies. The first step was to merge the two operations into a single team.

James informed George of the meeting. He quickly knew he had trouble on his hands when he received a very short email from George stating that he "didn't see the need to go all the way to England" and wasn't going to send any of his managers as they were "needed in China."

This was followed by multiple emails and phone conversations all without resolution or closure. Throughout the unpleasant process George was firm that this was his company and that the British facility was James's company. (Ouch.)

Of course, all of this found James on an airplane heading for China. He arranged a general meeting with George, Pete, and all the managers. When he arrived, he was shocked to find that George was not only NOT preparing to leave China, but was in fact building a new home. A western home built in China is something of a luxury, but George was convinced he had "earned it" and he was "paying for it."

James found out later that his salary was paying for some of it, however, the company paying for the monthly payments on the mortgage in addition to major upgrades. Since this was "his" operation and "his" company and "he" sacrificed everything for "his" right of position, George was sure he was making the proper decision.

In this case it was clear that George elevated himself to "King George I." He even hired his relatives to help him assure his actions were justified. ("King George II & III?")

Let's pause here for a moment and reflect on the overall issues James and his company were faced with: Let's put some of these experiences to work for you by outlining a few key actions that SHOULD have been completed.

It's apparent that the errors James made were as follows:

1. This was a classic case of sending someone who had the necessary technical skills but lacked the ability to adjust to different cultures (both corporate and country).

2. Sending (or using) a person who lacked the ability to adjust to a different perspective and to DIFFERENT BUSINESS PRACTICES was a huge no-no.

A person's success in both technical and existing business culture does not necessarily guarantee they will be successful in maneuvering in a different one. The two aren't necessarily transferable. For instance, just because a person was successful negotiating a contract in India it doesn't mean that he will be successful negotiating a contract in Russia.

As in the "King George" example we can reflect on both the Hybrid and King Effect that can (and will) occur over time on an international assignment. It is important to observe otherwise often overlooked behaviors in the Expat (or potential employee) before a hiring decision is made. Time is key, but mistakes can be costly. (As we have just seen.)

More importantly, in order to avoid the Hybrid and King Effects altogether, it's up to your ability to define, develop, and organize a long-term plan for these potential Expats.

THE CROWNING OF KING GEORGE I...

In James's case he took the short-term solution and found himself in a long-term problem. This could have been avoided with a tad more forethought, research, and observation.

I don't believe there is a defined "right-way" to hire or otherwise deal with Expats. Unfortunately, there is no specific, technical, "how to do it" manual for the global manager. However, I *do* think there are some guidelines we can follow (and modify along the way) to help us get the results we desire. As we have seen, managing an Expat is a lot more complex than managing a person in your own country.

SUCCESS IS 4 STEPS AWAY

Let's discuss some critical management issues with an Expat. From my experience (I'm talking both success and failures) these are the *minimum* actions that you need to develop, and they include 4 steps: (1) Develop a Training Plan (2) Hire the Right Person, (3) Conduct on-going Evaluations, and (4) Finishing it up.

Developing a Training Plan

When it comes to hiring an Expat, planning truly IS everything. To begin, writing down your key strategic objectives is critical to the Expat's success, as well as yours. These objectives must never be forgotten and constantly reviewed to ensure everyone is on the same road and has the same EXPECTATIONS.

If your organization has an H.R. Department but has NO international Human Resource experience, it will be up to you to ensure this critical step is developed to meet the objectives with an INTERNATIONAL perspective. This means that if your support staff does not have any international experience then you must do it yourself or find someone who can. Developing a training program by a department or individual with little or no international experience is a sure road to trouble, and the time you spend handling matters yourself will be well-spent, if one considers the alternatives.

Over 25 years ago (before I started my own company) I was working for a company who was opening up South America. It was a large organization which had not just one but several HR Departments.

Despite the number of HR staff, however, apparently few of them took time to write: The total amount of training designed to prepare the new, international employee was written on less than two pages. They didn't even address cultural differences, let alone solutions. Instead it "suggested" a language class at a local college, which was eventually cancelled due to lack of students, and gave the standard lecture on "corporate dress code."

Granted, times have changed and there is certainly a different level of awareness to cultural considerations today then there were five years ago, let alone twenty-five years ago. However, there was still a huge lack in effective training for the prospective international employee.

If you are a small businessperson you may be saying to yourself, "I cannot afford any such training." Also, you might be the only employee in your up and coming company, in which case you are *everything*. There are plenty of things you can do to prepare yourself, in the latter case, and your employees, in the former.

Where to begin? I would suggest you start with your local "World Trade Center." A number of them are qualified to give you some assistance (about 20% are certified to do more than just serve lunches). Even if they can't help you, the WTC has a lot of knowledge about other organizations that *could* help your specific needs. When in doubt: Call and ask. There are organizations in cities that are specifically related to your country of choice. Again: Call and ask.

Phone shy? Use the Internet. I am certainly not going to write about this communication tool, except to say that if you're not using this tool on a daily basis then you better reconsider doing *anything* on a global scale, let alone making money. Global Business moves and changes rapidly and you need the Internet to stay informed.

It really doesn't make any difference if you are a one person business or a large organization. You need to develop a training plan based around the company's overall objectives. Don't have any? Write it down. Develop a plan.

If you have the support of an H.R. Department be sure you get involved with the process of its development. Global training plans are much different than a regional plan, and you can't simply cross out Atlanta, Georgia and replace it with Georgia, Russia, and call that your "global plan."

Many of you may want a "template" or a written plan you can extract and start the training tomorrow. (I know I sure did.) Unfortunately, it's not that easy. Every company has different needs and every country has different cultural, economic, and contractual requirements. You have to bite the bullet and do it yourself. If you have some big bucks hire a specialist and have them design it for you, although personally I don't recommend this step.

Why not? You know your company the best and you know what you want, not some outside consultant. Write it down. Then start adding cultural consideration requirements for the country of choice. Don't know what they are? Start talking to people and ask questions. Talk to an HR Department manager if you want to formalize the format of your newly developed program. As I mentioned earlier, the internet provides an amazing amount of information to assist you with your creative new program.

There is simply no short cut for a good program. Even if you know the "perfect" person to do the job and they have the experience, the know-how and cultural sensitivity, develop the program anyway. It's your road map as well as the employee's. In addition to serving that particular purpose, it will also be the basis of your agreement between the two of you. Carry it around with you and review it. Compare the expectations with the actual performance you observe. Did it fulfill your expectations? If not, why? If not, change it and start follow up training. Stay involved throughout the process.

As we have seen, it's the only way to avoid the Hybrid and King Effects ...

HIRING THE RIGHT PERSON

Your training program is finished. What do you do now? Now you move to the next step: Finding the "right" person. As I have mentioned, you need to know more about this person than the "normal" processes can give. It's critical you know as much as possible to avoid obstacles to your future success, personally and professionally. As you begin to research your ideal recruit, keep in mind these following few items you need to carefully consider:

Communication Ability

Whoever you hire, they must be driven to communicate. If this person were put into a situation where they only knew a few words of the foreign language, they would still show enthusiasm in their communication skills and convey that with the client, the manager, the workers.

Communication, as we all know, shows up as both verbal and non-verbal. Simple gestures, hand movements, eye contact and body language all play a critical roll in communicating our desired ideas. Some of these skills can be taught; some are inherent. What you're looking for, ideally, is a combination of both.

If your prospective employee only holds sound technical skills but communicated poorly with foreign nationals, that's a sure sign you won't be able to use him. How do you know before the decision is made? One way to find out is to get involved with a local business organization related to your country of choice. Take your prospective employee to one of these meetings and see how they interact. Are they comfortable or uncomfortable? Insecure or overconfident? Too American or too condescending? This will be a dress rehearsal for the real thing and it will answer a lot of questions.

I believe in getting your "hands-dirty" or, in other words, "getting involved" at the lowest possible level. Oftentimes, this means leaving the comfort of your office for the factory floor. If you want to know why your productivity in a factory is low, try taking a day and follow the employees all the way through their day doing what they are doing. Often the results can be surprising: I found on one occasion that the food we supplied to our workers was terrible. By changing the quality of food our production rate went up 23% within the first week.

The lesson here is clear: Communicate by doing.

On another occasion, before hiring a new plant manager, I had a dinner arranged and invited about 50 employees who where being recognized for excellent performance. During the dinner, I noticed the prospective plant manager avoided the workers and never talked to one of them all night. Even though his resume was impressive I didn't hire him due to the lack of communication skills (he was an Australian being considered for the manager of a medical instrumentations factory).

It was quickly apparent that he wasn't the individual I needed due to the lack of cross cultural communication skills that I wanted to exist. As we all know, some things that look great on paper don't translate well to the factory floor.

Cultural Willingness

This is the area that I stress the most. Let's assume your prospective employee has the technical expertise that is necessary to "do the job." Is that enough? Not necessarily. The willingness to "experiment" within the culture is necessary for professional growth and cultural politeness. This could mean "eating what they eat" or attempting to communicate with their language or even discovering the etiquette of the proper way to drink certain teas. Whatever the case may be, it is critical that the individual has a driven curiosity with the culture and is willing to immerse him or herself both personally and professionally.

Unfortunately, when working abroad, it's simply impossible to "leave your work at the office." Our "work" is getting to know the people we live amongst, work with, and in many cases sell to. Eating dinner, having tea, or even just walking down the street may not seem like work, but when you or your employee can use this time to pick up cultural colloquialisms and use those in the workplace, we all benefit.

As with anything, too much of a good thing can be a bad thing: The particular caution I have with this "necessity" is that the Expat who embraces this with enthusiasm – perhaps I should say "too much" enthusiasm – is usually the one who falls quickly into the Hybrid Effect. What could make an Expat effective can (and will) be the ruin of him or her as well.

Let's not confuse this "willingness" as a reasoning that the Expat is in a foreign country in the first place. This is not the case. The willingness I talk about is the curiosity of learning and experiencing a different culture and a different point of view.

Cultural Viewpoint

I separate this aspect of an employee's effectiveness from "cultural willingness" because I have seen Expats out there "drinking sake with the boys" but then turn around and verbally criticize the cultural point of view when it suits his or purposes. This is a damaging (and can be somewhat staggering) characteristic of an international employee.

Cultural viewpoint is an attitude of what I call "live and let live." It's not an embracing of a culture, but instead the basic respect of cultural differences that inherently exist between Westerners and those they work amongst. This is critical for the international employee. I don't focus this just on the Expat, of course, but on any employee that has any interaction with another culture.

Just because someone is willing or is living in a different cultural tableau doesn't necessarily mean they are a healthy global citizen. It could mean any number of things, to the fact that they're running away from something, or someone, back in the states or simply experiencing a case of "the grass is always greener." Neither is a characteristic I would find admirable in my employees.

Finding this characteristic within an individual is difficult, if not next to impossible, on the first couple of interview cycles. It may be during a probationary period that it starts to surface, or during "field trips" like those I mentioned to employee ceremonies or the factory floor. The manager must ensure that during the probationary period situations will arise that will stress the candidate to make cultural decisions while you are observing their behavior.

Cultural Selling Skills

By now you are wondering why I am advocating selling skills for Expats or the international prospective employee. There are a lot of articles on the Internet regarding "how to…." They range from "negotiations" to getting one's cheese back in their pocket. All fun and somewhat helpful, but we're talking a major decision here and need the most help we can get.

In a global situation, *everyone* is part of the process, whether you call it negotiation or selling. Everyone must collaborate because there is such a cultural diversity when you are working with (selling ideas, products, getting better prices, delivery schedules, etc.) different belief systems.

It's important in your own country, of course, but downright *critical* in foreign countries. The Expat or the prospective international employee must have these critical skills. "Ah..." you are asking, "why does it matter if you are just looking for an IT manger or a technical manger?" This skill is important for ANY employee who is up for consideration for a foreign post.

Remember the old saying "practice makes perfect?" This is the case with cultural selling skills. Understanding cultural norms will have value and meaning only to those who practice.... and practice.... and practice. This is the "get your hands-dirty" approach.

Try this one yourself: Find a local organization that supports another country. Go talk to them. Try negotiating with them for practice. A number of organizations are there primarily to assist foreign businessmen to conduct business in their home country. What a great practice area to develop your own skills. Potentially you can incorporate employee training with speaking events, lunch meetings with foreign guests, and training seminars.

You certainly want your prospective new employee to have a collaborative approach and not a combative approach to sales/negotiation. When faced with different cultures its takes on a different course necessary for positive outcome, so that sales is not just a goal but a necessity, from the top to the bottom of the organization.

During a recent visit to my factories in China I came across a young man in his mid-thirties who was on a brief assignment in Southern China. I noticed that there wasn't just little cultural interaction, there was none: He was focused only on eating at the local Pizza Hut and certainly avoided getting into conversations with the local people. When the day was finished he would rush back to the Hilton Hotel for a western meal and then confine himself to his room till the next morning. How effective was he on his job? It mattered little: All of this pointed to short term results and long term failure, no matter how impressive his resume.

Proper screening will ensure that when quick decisions are necessary they can be made with confidence and experience. Choosing a good candidate for a potential international position will take more effort than a domestic position. It's no different than ordering from a foreign restaurant: It's easier to pick a Big

Mac over a Quarter Pounder because we're so familiar with them. But deciding between Pad Thai and Gum Shi takes a little more effort. Unfortunately, in the world of international business the stakes are a tad higher than ordering the wrong meal: The manager must consider other traits than those who make up their technical ability.

Some of these considerations are: Cross cultural communication ability, the willingness to experiment within different cultures, embracing different cultural viewpoints, and showing a strong ability to sell within other cultures.

ONGOING EVALUATIONS

Okay, so you finally found the "right" person and have developed a training program. Now what? With the financial commitment you have made to either ship yourself or someone else to a foreign country, it's the follow-up that will ensure you are keeping the "ship" on track.

Consistent communication, performance observations, formal evaluations, and periodic returns are all necessary to ensure your success. Unlike regional employees, these people are usually thousands of miles away in a foreign culture without the luxury of having corporate support in the next office.

Not only do they need to be the consummate self-starter, but they also need to possess those traits we listed above. And even if they do possess those traits, they can always benefit from your experience in such matters.

If not you, then someone: As much as the commitment is necessary for the employee the commitment of his immediate manager and the commitment of the corporation is critical for the mutual success.

Make travel a big part of your budget during this initial phase: It cannot be stressed enough that the employee must return on a regular frequency to the home country to prevent early rise of the Hybrid or the King Effect. This coupled with visits and consistent communications (live voice please – email doesn't count – video conferencing is the best) will ensure not only an open line of communication but likewise a willingness to communicate.

The employee *must* interact with his peers as well as his manager. This provides the necessary cross-pollination of ideas and to strengthening the home connection.

When developing the employee's overall plan and the objectives continue the process with examples of evaluations. This gives everyone a clear picture of expectations and goals. With employees so far away from the corporate culture, it is easily forgotten that what quickly happens back at headquarters takes a defined effort to communicate the feelings to the employees who are "out in left field."

When everyone is under one roof, it's easy to "assume" that all people know the company's current tempo. When you put an employee in another culture the tempo is NOT THE SAME. As a manager, you are responsible for bridging this gap.

FINISHING THE JOB

In the face of hiring a successful Expat, most companies forget about what happens when you are going to bring the employee *back* to his home country. This is tricky and the stakes are high: As we've seen, this is when you have a 25% chance of losing the person you've worked so hard to hire, train, and retain. If you lose that person to a competitor, your loss is even greater than losing an employee – can you say, "trade secrets" – and could be tragic depending on the employee, the competitor, and the timing.

In the Harvard article they quoted a firm that lost all their mangers – all 25 of them – in a two-year period! They figure the loss to be $50 million, just tossed to the wind. I don't know about you, but I cannot afford that kind of a loss.

The same article pointed out that most companies do not have a position for the returning Expat. About a third were filling "temporary jobs" and over 60% said they lacked opportunities to put all their experience to work. You can see now why over 25% (average) leave after returning home. Poor planning and poor management are often the cause, and not always on behalf of the Expat.

I believe you cannot wait until the person returns, or even wait 6 months *before* they return. So when should you start? I recommend starting the planning stage *before* you even hire or promote the person. This gives you a better idea of the quality of individual you need. By doing this, it will assist the manager to develop a working relationship with the individual and help them WHILE they are on the overseas assignment. In addition to solving the problem of what the Expat will be doing when he returns, it's called "repatriation," but you also got to know where they are going as well as where the company is going – to help everyone achieve their goals.

Repatriation is a highly talked about subject within giant companies, but little is discussed within the small to medium companies. This is the inverse of how it should be: Big companies can afford little mistakes when it comes to repatriation, small to medium companies can afford *no* mistakes.

With globalization affecting everyone's business, large or small, we need to make our employee's career path part of the company's vision. This is why it's important to develop this right when you start working on the company's objectives. When you put your pen to paper it must encompass the employee's career along with the company's vision and objectives. They cannot work at cross purposes.

Want some more information on repatriation? Read on.

REPATRIATION NATION

The retention of corporate professionals after a global assignment is key to the future success of your global organization. Why? Because these returning employees now have information on the culture and the integration of corporate goals to share with your employees back at headquarters. This assists in developing a successful formula for the TOTAL organization. How can you minimize the challenges that your repatriated employees face after returning from an overseas assignment? How can the knowledge they have learned abroad be transferred and shared? Here are a few ideas:

1. **Culture Shock Coming Home.** This is a highly discussed topic and an amazing amount of data has been collected on this subject. Until fairly recently, the idea of offering training to professionals who were coming home was considered odd at best, and unnecessary at worst. Repatriates were often thrown back into their jobs (or temporary jobs with no career path) with no discussion of their international assignments. Research has shown that a home culture can seem strange after having spent a period of time negotiating a new culture. I even find that a few months away from home gives me a strange sense of the surrounding environment when I arrive at home. (Imagine what it might feel like to an employee!)

   Providing repatriates with an outlet to discuss their feelings can be crucial to successful repatriation. Even talking to their family helps, though talking to another company employee is the best for all involved. I would even suggest having the previous Expat to be responsible for the repatriation program upon his or her return. It really helps when someone who is conducting the program already has a sensitivity of what you have just been through. They've already been there and it makes the transformation for the "new Expat" easier.

2. **Becoming a Teacher.** Sound repatriate training should include time for the repatriate to discuss how to transfer the knowledge he or she has learned. This may best be done on an informal, just-in-time basis during a special project, or during meetings with the boss, or during special meetings of their team. This is one topic that should be included in the job requirement.

   No matter what the Expat may have accomplished abroad, now the company's asset is what is between that person's ears. Downloading to a number of people is the best. Transfer of knowledge becomes different for many different jobs. It could be just a white paper for the company newsletter or conducting training sessions for other employees. It should also include having this person assist in the job development of the next Expat and his or her repatriation when the time comes. In addition to the individual, I would include the spouse and the children. A spouse who has been through the process knows what to expect and can help the other family quickly adjust. They can become a critical member to helping the family adjust to their environment. A happy family produces a happy, adjusted, employee. Remember: When it comes to repatriation, don't forget the spouse.

3. **Mentoring Others.** The repatriate can serve a key role in helping the organization develop a global workforce by serving as a mentor to expatriates going to the same country or part of the world. By handing the "baton" to the next Expat, this provides a sense of purpose for the individual and ensures that the company obtains a "return on their investment."

   The information exchange between the repatriate and expatriate can help ensure a positive experience for the expatriate by alerting him or her to the challenges faced when working abroad. This mentorship can be extended to the younger workers by providing education and extend the company's globalization sensitivity. (This is really a nice statement for getting more business, ensuring profitability, and managing cost.) Mentoring may help the repatriate too, but its real value is payback time for the company. Transferring this knowledge is critical for the long term growth of the organization.

4. **Outside the Company.** Organizing a group of repatriates who can share their knowledge of international business during regularly scheduled presentations gives a clear signal to all employees that global experience is valued. In

addition, the networking between repatriates can help your organization build a more satisfied global workforce. This is a lot of nice words, of course, but what it really means is to get out and into other organizations and start sharing cultural ideas.

The successful employee can now become your company's "goodwill ambassador" and provide necessary public relations that would not be available without his/her experience. Have them speak at organizations and join cross-cultural sensitive organizations (remember the World Trade Organization?). Getting involved outside the company's boundary requires careful HR considerations to ensure confidentiality, but ensures gains for the company's future that you can bank on for years to come.

5   **Their Future.** Who wants an uncertain future? Especially when facing a difficult and challenging role overseas. The strain and uncertainty of the overseas assignment can be reduced when the expatriate knows what career opportunities are available upon his or her return. This knowledge can also create a much smoother transition once the employee returns home. This is easier said than done, no doubt, but set the intention at the start and develop a career path so that the Expat returns home to more than an empty promise – and a temp job. Yes, things change and the global market is quick. One earthquake in India can change the way we do business in China or South America. However, our employees need a sense of direction to maintain their loyalty (besides making more money).

To remain competitive globally, organizations need to make it clear to all employees, and not just your Expats, that global experiences are encouraged. One way to do that is through an organizational design that promotes – and even rewards – international assignments. Repatriate training programs are part of the overall program.

Too often, repatriate professionals leave their organizations because they feel that their knowledge is undervalued. Thoughtful planning is necessary to ensure the company – and the employee(s) – will be rewarded in the long term.

Finding the "Right" Person

As many books, seminars, lectures, classes, opinions, arguments, reviews, termination letters, employment contracts and emails that have been written about this topic there are just as many opinions. In some companies there is even an entire department dedicated to this, and only this, subject. You may have heard of them: They are called Human Resource Departments. They generate employee manuals, memos, instructions, directions, and job descriptions among other important aspects for their company.

I am amazed at how much information is out there for this purpose. Colleges even offer degrees that center around the goal of finding and retaining the right employee. And though the sheer amount of information can often be overwhelming, it really boils down to the person who is doing the hiring.

Do you really have all the necessary information to make an informed decision? Don't kid yourself; it's tough and sometimes all that is left is your intuition. I am certainly not going to start outlining a "how to do it" manual on the fine art of hiring the perfect person for that job you are creating. (I'll save that for the sequel!)

With all the information out there, not to mention your unique knowledge of your unique company, it's really up to you. Just be sure that the global element is soundly embedded in your job description and your company's objectives and vision. Be sure you are committed to the process and development of this individual. You are only as good as the people you employ.

Now, to wrap up, let's get back to the story of George. Remember him? We left George when he proclaimed (himself, that is) to be "King George I." By this time, George's wife now had her two sisters working for George, a third sister was loaned company money to setup a business along with a $5,000 dollar loan to her *brother*! The watchdog (or so James thought) accountant was now making $8,000 dollars a month to watch the "books" for the Board Members.

George didn't care too much for Chinese food and was very selective with his meals. He went to great lengths to find western food and even, at times, prepared them himself. He even made it a practice to visit Hong Kong and go directly to the nearest western eatery.

Strangely enough he loved to eat barbequed chicken served on the sidewalks at various parts of the city and country. James commented that it was always a curiosity to see this strange man hunched over munching on street side chicken while wailing at the merchant about western values.

It was during one such sidewalk meeting that James found King George I with his classic baseball hat, shorts, sandals, and scruffy white beard. While hunched over munching on his chicken in one hand, continually smoking with the other, he was expounding to James the necessity of giving him "funding to expand the business." During this time he was proud to show James his newly built western home, new car with his full time driver while at the same time giving money to his brother-in-law.

James realized the person he knew a short six-years prior had officially morphed into "King George I." All in all, the mistakes he made over the years with managing this person had accumulated into "King George," a strange man that is no longer culturally accepted in either country. Listening to James I could not help to think of the classic Frankenstein novel; the person (monster?) that he created was now haunting him.

James knew that he had to cut the ties between himself and King George and he wasn't clear on the method. His concern was that a portion of the company's business now depended on the factory that George had set up and was currently operating. The balance, however, was easily transferable.

Over the next eight months, he successfully separated George and his followers from his business (nice words for "firing them"). He then spun off the factory that George created over the years and packaged it into a potentially sellable asset. Knowing full well of the loss, it was important to remove George from further damaging the balance of the company.

James offered the company at a great discount to George and his followers. They quickly took the offer and proceeded on their own. It has taken James over a year to clean up the damage that was done but in doing so his business increased over 20% and as a result he taught me a great deal by way of his colossal blunder: I have since been applying the lessons he shared with me on a daily basis.

The blame can be shared, in this case: The issue with George was not all George's problem. As you can tell, the situation was mismanaged from the start. Early mistakes compounded later on into a situation that was not acceptable to anyone. James learned a lesson to go on to become a better global manager. Fortunately, it didn't cost James as much as it could have and it did cause a major cleaning of company which, in turn, gave James a burst of wonderful energy that he is still enjoying to this day.

James now has closer communications with the company's employees, higher profit levels, expanded markets, and better cost controls. The rise and fall of King George I truly *was* a blessing in disguise.

It is important for the reader to read these simple lessons over a few times. It is important to see the many mistakes that were made and to learn from them. If you can avoid just one of these, the price you paid to read this book will be well worth the investment.

PARTING WORDS

This chapter should not discourage the reader from considering using an Expat, but should make the reader realize that their responsibility must increase to reduce the high failure rate of the traditional Expat, according to the author's personal experience and those recorded for posterity in the annals of business journals everywhere.

Likewise, the manager must acknowledge the necessary increase of the time required to help make the Expat a success. In fact, I find that most of the failures occur when the manager **assumes** that the potential Expat has the "experience" necessary and then displays typical supervisory practices associated with non-global managers.

What's wrong with this scenario?

Well, we all know what happens when we **assume** …

EPILOGUE:

Facing the Future – Is the World Moving To China?

T-shirts, piggy banks, toys, ashtrays, lighters, computer chips, gumballs. As we buy products, consume electronics, read articles, discuss topics, and even read the back of milk cartons about the various world economies, we often find ourselves asking a common question: What *isn't* made in China?

China has certainly emerged as the key global manufacturing center for a wide range of product. Today, there is virtually no wholesaler, retailer or OEM in the modern world that is not sourcing some, if not all, of its products from China.

The advantages of a low cost production site or a cluster of suppliers with an ever growing, fast moving market has created opportunities for entrepreneurs all over the world, and I have tried to share a variety of those with you here in this book.

As we have seen, the world has certainly changed and nowhere is that fact more evident than in the ever-shifting face of the global marketplace. It seems that "made in Hong Kong" has move to "made in Taiwan" to "made in China," with the emerging possibility to "made in India." What will those labels show us? Has this process stopped? Who will emerge as the next big "made in" manufacturer?

During the 80's and 90's I witnessed a flood of Hong Kong, Taiwanese and Korean businessmen move their operations to China. As the cost of manufacturing increased in their homelands, coupled with a more competitive global marketplace, the advantages of such a move were obvious. Lowering production costs and giving relief to their shrinking profit margins demanded outsourcing of their mass-market manufacturing operations, and forward thinking companies responded quickly.

Those who didn't, more than likely, are no longer in business ...

By the late 1990's even small to medium businesses began pulling their heads out of their domestic turf and began looking at manufacturing opportunities in China. But the migration is far from over: Mounting pressures on operational costs continues into our new century.

The continuation of their shrinking profits and intense competition from outside forces has forced the small to medium businessman out of developed countries to survive. This is most apparent with companies that have products that lack dynamic innovation and/or reduced research and development successes.

But that isn't the whole story, of course. Further study into the reasons behind this wave of small businesses to China reveals the following considerations:

- Appreciation in domestic currency producing a lack of competitiveness in the global marketplace;

- Strong domestic currency makes it more convenient to invest into China;

- Operating with a fixed rate of exchange avoids exchange rate fluctuations;

- As more and more countries join the EU, wages and production cost increase, making China more appealing;

- Lack of human resources (textile factories, wood production, etc.);

- Products that lack innovation to upgrade must move closer to China to reduce cost;

- China labor force tends to be more productive (Vietnamese and Indian wages are generally lower);

- Availability of suppliers are more abundant in China;

- Client factories are moving to China, thereby pulling other support factory to the same locations (passive full-in factor, VMI and JIT program demands, etc.);

- Chinese manufacturers are now effective competitors, which sell cheaper on the global market;

Chinese local manufacturers have also started to manufacture state-of-the-art products and are quickly becoming internationally recognized (along with patents and designs). As a result, the small to medium businessman is forced to delocalize to lower costs in order to sustain growth and/or profit margins. Consequently, entry into China via acquisitions of existing suppliers or competitors will gain even more momentum in the future.

This is all academic, of course, and through experience I've learned that it's often easier to understand these issues in real time than in black in white. Let's consider two different conversations I had with a competitor of mine to further emphasize this global migration to China.

This particular businessperson manufactured a low-tech product family, specifically power chords. It certainly was not an innovative product, by any means. In fact, there was no research and development department at his company whatsoever. The product "standards" were established by corresponding country safety codes, thereby not affording much innovation.

Over the course of several years, manufacturing moved to various countries to reduce production cost and labor. These products face an uncertain future with shrinking margins and no other country offering a solution. Survival comes only from innovation of supply (JIT, Reducing distance to customers, JV with raw material suppliers, etc.).

This particular businessperson was salvaged only by getting acquired by another company wishing to by-pass all necessary process, procedures, and training required to open a factory in China. In this case, both parties were successful. Unfortunately, the selling company was sold for only a fraction of what it could have realized if the company put more effort into expanding to other products (thereby innovating profitable solutions).

I'm having more and more conversations like the one I had with this particular businessperson. A new wave of acquisitions will begin to occur with companies beginning to discover what their competitors have already deduced: That it is cheaper and faster to acquire companies already doing business in the foreign country of choice.

It makes sense, right? I mean, why reinvent the wheel when somebody, in this case an already established company, has already done it for you?

There are some choices a company can make when it comes to investing in a manufacturing operation in China. Generally speaking (acquiring or starting from scratch) the most used vehicles are: Wholly Foreign Owned Enterprises (WFOE's), Joint Ventures (JV'S) and Processing and Assembly Factories (LLJG). The LLJG's are the most popular since the late 1970's. Let's take a look at the pros and cons of each in the following section:

LLJG's

During the early years of global expansion (which current theory credits to the 1970's), this method was very popular with investors from Hong Kong and Taiwan primarily because it did not require setting up an entity on its own rights, and yet it was just good enough to entrust a local factory to manufacture products for export. Today this is still a possibility if you only want to export the manufactured products and do not want to setup a full fledged WFOE.

Actually, LLJG's means processing and assembling of imported/ supplied material or parts. Basically, you ship the materials to this factory (foreign materials), use the low cost labor to assemble and then export (only) the finished product. Basically, this is all the LLJG can perform. So if you want to use domestic materials or sell to the domestic markets ... forget this method.

It is important to remember before selecting this method that the LLJG does *not* have a legal status. It is merely an "arrangement" between a Chinese partner and the foreign investor.

Usually, the investor supplies the equipment free of charge to the Chinese partner (equipment is entered duty free and VAT free for a certain period of time). Any materials shipped by the investor are considered "bonded" and thus do not attract VAT or custom duties. The end-product must be 100% exported and NO domestic sales are allowed.

So, considering those factors, the advantages of this method are:

- No capital required;

- No need to invest in buildings;

- No VAT;

- Multiple production of different products are allowed;

- Equipment imported is custom and VAT free;

- Production contract is short; thereby allowing flexibility;

On the other hand, the disadvantages include:

- No domestic sales allowed;

- Income tax is assessed by the tax bureau;

- Bonded goods are closely monitored by authorities (get used to visitors);

- You must rely on good relationship with the Chinese party;

- No VAT rebates;

- Very rigid structure;[35]

---

35   Shira D., 2004 Business Guide to Shanghai and the Yangtze River Delta (China Briefing Media, Ltd) 2003

If you are looking to acquire a business I would certainly think twice before I would purchase a LLJG facility. Also, I do think this type of vehicle (LLJG) will be phased out in the future as the primary function of the LLJG arrangement is to exploit low cost labor for the foreigner. With the new WFOE regulations being considered, the function of the LLJG for the Chinese will, most likely, be avoided.

WFOE

This vehicle is becoming the most popular and certainly one of the most widely used in China. To fulfill its commitment to the WTO, China is opening up more and more industry sectors allowing this type of vehicle to the foreign businessman.

As mentioned in Chapter 2, this is one of the more important vehicles to keep your eye on. China is changing rapidly and it's important for the prudent businessman to "get their hands dirty."

WFOE's negate the requirement for a Chinese partner and do not require a large amount of capital to fund. Basically, WFOE's are Limited Liability Companies under Chinese law. The shareholders are 100% foreign, usually a single international business who owns 100% of the stock.

Registered Capital is a requirement and the amount will depend on your industry as well as the regional location. For example, a WFOE establishing in Shanghai will be faced with a larger capital requirement than Shenzhen.

A Simple Rep Office

If you don't wish to manufacture but you still want a presence in China, then a simple Rep Office, or RO, may be the initial answer to your problem. RO's are useful and inexpensive. Don't think it's simple to setup, however; it's not. As with WFOE's and other vehicles, I would strongly suggest a good legal or accounting firm to assist you through this vital process.

Why an RO office? The reasons are as multi-faceted as the process of setting one up: For starters, they can perform a number of tasks for you. They can be helpful in facilitating trade between your headquarters and other Chinese entities in China. Remember, however, that RO's cannot invoice for service or sales in China directly. They can, however, introduce business to your headquarters or act as a liaison in administrative and sales matters.

There are some taxes that may apply to your industry and you also must hire local staff via an organization known as FESCO. Be forewarned: Other requirement may apply, such as the submission of monthly reports, annual audits, licenses, and registration for taxes as a few examples. RO licenses are usually good for 2-3 years, but are renewable.

The application process is somewhat bureaucratic and administrative and is a combination of Documentation Requirements and Application Procedures. It may still cost you (besides the setup fees) some taxation, which could amount to about 10% of the operation cost of the Rep Office.

Despite its drawbacks, however, the Rep Office License is a good one if you wish to have a local presence to manage services or manage goods you are buying. In simple language, it is one step above being an importer/broker. This gives you a location in China and can assist with cross cultural differences.

GETTING CREATIVE:

Let's Consider Intellectual Property Protection

Companies outsourcing manufacturing to China are rightfully concerned about how to effectively protect their Intellectual Property, or IP, rights. Disregard for IP rights in China is a systematic problem, and unfortunately the judicial system there has not caught up with the needs of the business community.

The important thing to remember is that the Chinese legal system does provide some protection for IP rights and the foreign company can take advantage of the various protections available.

Patents, trademarks, copyrights, and integrated circuit layout designs can all – and should – be registered. Trade secrets, though broadly and vaguely defined, are also protectable. Other common sense measures of protecting your IP rights include choosing your business partners carefully, building good relationships with the Chinese IP enforcement agencies, and monitoring the marketplace for potential products that might be infringing on those rights.

Even though there have been significant improvements to the IP laws within China, the foreign businessperson *must* seek legal advice before making critical decisions abroad. Fortunately, there are a number of good attorneys that specialize in IP law within China. Find a good one and register with the appropriate government agency.

GETTING YOUR HANDS DIRTY

Globalization has become a great boon for the so-called consultant. I have seen short-term businesspeople hanging up their consultant sign only to find that the laws, regulations, or that key mentor disappearing the following morning. It is important to know that the rapid changes in business laws in foreign countries are not only considerable but constant. Business practices change faster than the wind (and are sometimes even less predictable).

Rather than hiring a consultant I would suggest you consult one of three prime sources. You should first look at (1) existing businessmen who are "in the trenches" on a daily basis. This is your best source for a mentor relationship. These individuals are learning every day, even after years of experience. These individuals are invaluable.

(2) Local agencies and organizations (U.S. Commerce Departments, World Trade Centers, etc.) are a great source of

information and can provide contact information as well as technical support.

(3) I don't mean to make a blanket accusation of all foreign trade consultants. There *are* some "consultants" out there that *can* be a good source, *if* you are careful. Personally, I would suggest considering only those who have had over 10 years of experience inside of China (not the casual visitor or passing academic with lofty degrees and no street experience) and have on-going business contracts with similar companies to yours.

For my money, though, as you might have figured out by now, nothing beats "getting your hands dirty." You can only read so much, talk so much, and listen to enough people until it will be up to you to make the ultimate and final decision.

You must get on the plane and immerse yourself in the culture, the people, and their laws in order to become an effective entrepreneur. A few months of experience only makes the person dangerous (when someone says "I know China..." be very wary). Your commitment must be ongoing to bridge the cultural gap.

YOU'VE HEARD WHAT I'M THINKING, BUT ...

What are the Chinese Thinking?

The Chinese mainland has become one of the world's most popular investment destinations, as its economy continues to open and becomes increasingly market-oriented. With this ongoing development, overseas investment is playing an increasingly pivotal role in determining the nation's economic progress.

The Chinese Academy of International Trade and Economic Co-Operation, a think-tank of the Ministry of Commerce, recently completed a report on overseas investment trends from 2005 to 2007 after six months of research in order to gain an insight into trends related to Foreign Direct Investment (FDI) in China, as well as local investment policies.

In summary, the report estimates that more investments are expected in the allotted time span. The report mainly covers multinationals listed in the Top 1,000 from America, Japan, South Korea, Hong Kong, Taiwan and Europe. I am sure you are now wondering why this would be of interest to the small to medium size business. Well, it primarily shows where the supply of raw materials will be offered, so it may show where your customer will be located. More than likely, it *will* show you where your market is located.

Either way, without a doubt, the Chinese are all set to welcome more overseas investment in the years to come. They expect (from the contents of this report) that 82 percent of the companies surveyed that the companies will boost their investment inside of China. Along with this, they report that production, sales, and technology development are all increasing.

Most large Multinationals inside of China usually form a JV until they establish a foothold in the country. Once they show moderate success, they then begin to consolidate their investment and start to move the product from their own country to China. Their edge is in terms of capital, network, market knowledge, technology and information.

During this developmental stage you will see the Multinational begin to reap profit only to turn around and reinvest aggressively. This is the stage China believes it is entering. How does this all affect you? Well, this stage will "drag" many other small to medium companies along. Basically, the "road is being paved" for the smaller business. Suppliers are becoming abundant, consumers are more educated, and information is more accessible. The small to medium businesses must enter into the foreign marketplace to remain competitive in their own country.

(*SOMETIMES*) SIZE DOES MATTER

I am a big believer in small businesses but, sometimes, the big companies provide the "horse-power" to open the gates for the rest of us. In the case of China, it has already happened.

The key for us to understand about those implications for the future is that the expansion of the large multinational is their market scale and high growth of their Chinese industries. Let's take the IT and automotive industries as an example; the mainland IT market accounted for 30.8 percent of the Asian market in 2003 and is expected to increase to 38% by 2005 and continue to outstrip the global IT industry's average. [36]

Using this example, the small to medium businesses that support or service the IT markets have an excellent growth opportunity in China, primarily due to the large multinational company expansion. Therefore, as a small businessman keeping your eye on the large multinationals in your own sectors can provide the necessary insight when developing your own strategy for foreign expansion. You can – and must – apply this to any industry sectors.

China is set to open up its market to an unprecedented extent and has created many new opportunities for overseas investment in this period (2005) thanks to the Chinese government's fulfillment of its pledges made upon joining the World Trade Organization in 2002.

I would expect the Multinationals will begin setting up more retail outlets as the mainland frees up the commercial distribution sectors. When? I would expect the later part of 2005 or 2006, if all goes as planned.

This would stimulate growth and should be carefully looked at for your primary strategy. Waiting beyond 2006 may cause the interested businessman considerable loss of opportunity and revenue.

RESEARCH & DEVELOPMENT:

Necessary and Growing

China is beginning to see the Multinationals (over 61 percent, actually) increase their Research & Development (R & D)

---

36   Shira D., 2004 Business Guide to Shanghai and the Yangtze River Delta (China Briefing Media, Ltd) 2003

spending. However, the reasons (so the report I mentioned in the previous section discovered) for this include:

- Only some R&D efforts are transferred to the overseas facility. The core R&D functions are retained at home;

- R&D investments are shifting toward mergers and acquisitions;

- R&D in mainland China is focusing on local applications rather than elementary studies;

Consider further that the multinational still holds the fundamental R&D at the home office. This type of R&D requires more skilled professionals and is critical to the future of the company. The Multinationals are reluctant to move basic R&D outside of their home country for a variety of reasons, not the least of which being that it's easier to keep secrets in their own headquarters.

The point to this discussion is that R&D is growing in China. It may not necessarily be the fundamental type your company or mine is used to, but it is still R&D focused on applications. I believe, also, that it will take at least another decade before China will produce a Nobel Prize winner that is "home-grown." This movement, however, is a critical turning point in moving toward stronger Intellectual Property Laws, which I believe are vital to most Western companies.

Businesspeople are beginning to become more comfortable with R&D protection. By the end of 2004, overseas companies had established over 700 R&D centers in China. [37]Looking at these centers, it quickly becomes evident that there are some fundamental differences in "why" they set them up in China. However, all of them express a level of comfort in protecting their innovations. In fact, 33 percent plan on increasing the number of projects for their centers.

As always, I must give caution to these considerations: It is vitally important that you carefully plan and organize your strategy before implementation. The numbers are impressive, but progress is slow.

---

37 United States Central Intelligent Agency, The World Fact Book (U.S. Government) 2004

SOLE OWNERSHIP PREVAILS

So what is the preferred method of global expansion in Asia? Shifting from Joint Ventures to solely-funded manufacturing facilities is becoming apparent as a popular means of doing business in China. Most (about 57 percent) of the Multinationals favor this shift and are becoming more comfortable in cooperating with the local governments and local suppliers. [38]

It is interesting to note that about 25% of the Multinationals that were surveyed for the recent report said they are "considering acquisitions of local companies to boost this cross-cultural relationship." Obviously, these companies are obtaining a better understanding of mainland markets through their long-term participation.[39]

The recent revisions of Wholly Foreign Own Enterprises (WFOE) rules are lifting many restrictions on the prospective businessman. This includes the service sectors as well as the manufacturing sectors.

I believe that the new changes in the WFOE rules will give a boost to China as well as an opportunity to the small to medium foreign business person. If you are considering China for either an opportunity to expand your market and/or an opportunity to control cost, NOW is a great time to take action.

LOCATION, LOCATION, LOCATION!

So, where should the Entrepreneur in Asia set-up shop? As in all areas of real estate, the answer is simple: Location, location, location! To that end, the areas of investment revolve around a few general areas in China. In order of popularity, they include:

---

38   Shira D., 2004 Business Guide to Shanghai and the Yangtze River Delta (China Briefing Media, Ltd) 2003
39   Ibid

1. The Yangtze River Delta (47%);

2. The Bohai Economic Rim (22%);

3. The Pearl River Delta (21%);

4. Northwest, Western and Central China (8 – 9 %);

Most foreign companies are investing in the development zones within these areas. However, I believe that stability of the local government, policies and how we can practically apply our business are the major issues with businesspeople in China.

Local governments play an important part with your business. However, China must ensure that local government be transparent, efficient, and keep their promises to the prospective businessman.

Sometimes we can think that such promises are too good to be true, which raises concerns about the reliability of the statements. As a prospective businessman in China, your diligence in research, relationships, and careful evaluations are critical before committing investments, no matter what the location.

The (High) Cost of Information

Most foreign businessmen that I talked to in China consider "information" to be the primary (critical) factor in their success. Information in and about China is not free. In fact, the cost of obtaining information about your industry, market, human resources and policies in China is relatively high. This, coupled with the typical foreigner's limited knowledge about the region and its customs, challenges the manager's ability to perform his or her duties.

Unfortunately, there are no easy answers to these questions. As I pointed out in the previous chapters, you can't simply rely on a consultant or in-country research study to make major decisions about the future of your company.

You *must* be willing to get into the trenches and discover the facts for yourself. This includes working with other businesses, which can help you with actual, on-going experience. Thus the cost you will likely incur is not only in the form of money but also in your time and effort to extract the necessary information so you can make sound decisions.

FACING THE OBVIOUS

During my visits to my facilities in China, I try to exchange employees if only for a few days. Why? The answer is simple and fundamental to success: I find it very important and effective to have employees experience the cultural differences between the countries.

Early in 2005, I brought over a young manager for his first visit to the United States. Not only was the trip beneficial to this individual and myself, but it was a good eye-opener for everyone. He discovered a better way to communicate with the domestic office and even gave good suggestions on how we could handle the Chinese mind during periods of conflict and problem solving.

It was during this visit, in fact, that he began to search for a present for his young wife back home, who was pregnant. He wanted to bring home something made in the USA, as well as culturally representative of our country. During one of these weekend "hunts" we began to realize that most of the merchandise was, in fact, made in China and is only *marketed* here in the USA.

We also began to discuss the mass market that China is offering the world. China is a country that has over 20% of the world's population. It consumes more than 20% of the world's cell phones, 34% of the world's cigarettes, consumes 10% of the world's electricity, eats 19% of the world's chickens, eats 19% of the world's ice cream, buys over 23% of the world's production of televisions, uses over 32% of the world's cotton, and eats over 12% of the world's beef! As if that wasn't already amazing enough, it is widely known that these percentages are still growing. [40]

Wow.

---

40   United States Central Intelligent Agency, The World Fact Book (U.S. Government) 2004

What else can you say when presented with such staggering statistics?

WOW!!!

China is capitalizing on young students that are educated abroad who are bringing knowledge of finance, internet, technical R&D and innovative styles back to China. In fact, during 1997 (the latest figures I could find) over 65,000 Chinese students were studying abroad.

China, it seems, is both exited and cautious about their newly educated citizenry. I remember someone commenting that they are both excited and scared about creating another Bill Gates. I believe there is a very determined group of young people who see the future as limitless.

Sounds like the USA, doesn't it?

My accounting firm in China hires only Chinese who are educated overseas, which brings a richness in cultural diversity and effectiveness when working with foreign corporations. This is an example of what is happening in China. China is (and has been) on the move for some time now, and I believe the country is only picking up steam. So what do you want to do? Keep up with them now or play catch-up later?

My young Chinese manager continued to hunt for the "perfect" gift for his young, pregnant wife back home. The biggest problem was to find something in the USA that was not already "made in China."

Finally, during a visit to my small hometown we found a Native American Shop where he bought a pair of handmade moccasins. I wasn't sure where the leather came, from but I hoped that it was from North America and not "you know where."

A few weeks later, I was talking to the group who distributed the moccasins. To my surprise the moccasins were actually imported from Canada. The Canadian firm bought the leather from Argentina, the beads came from China, sewing thread from Australia and the workers were mainly from Vietnam (who had immigrated years prior). When all was said and done and the price tag affixed and the item was put on the shelves in the good old US of A, the product was from the "Americas" with a small splash from China after all (the beads).

It is important for the businessperson to recognize the importance for global marketing, global trade, global manufacturing and keep a global vision integrated within their business strategy. Understanding how it affects your business and where your opportunity exists is important for future growth in a global competitive market.

No longer do we just compete within a small geographic area. We now compete by selling our own products in different countries as well as our own. Like China itself, this prospect may excite you and, at the same time, scare you. But knowledge is power, and it is my hope that with the knowledge contained in this book I have given you the power to conquer that fear, and harness that excitement.

A WORD OF CAUTION

Obviously, this book arose from a specific need, that being the fact that there is currently a lot of interest in Asia these days, with China typically being the central point of the discussions. With all the books, articles, speeches and political focus pointed in the direction of the Land of the Rising Sun, however, we must not forget the rest of the world.

Yes, this book is primarily focused on Asia (as pointed out in the title). But it just as easily could have been titled the *Entrepreneur in South America* or the *Entrepreneur in Eastern Europe* or even the *Entrepreneur in Russia.* (And, if all goes well with this title, one day might be!)

As China progresses into a world class supply chain center, we must keep our eyes and ears on the rest of the world. It is easy to get caught up in all the excitement and furor over Asia, but we must be aware of the markets that are expanding rapidly in other countries. Although this makes good business sense, it is easy to overlook business opportunities when we are focused on China.

I remember how rare it was to see a western face in Asia during my first forays there in the 70s and 80s and even early 90s. It's not like that anymore, and that makes me wonder, "Where is the NEW Asia? Who will be the next world leader?"

After all you've learned about Asia in this book I'm certainly not suggesting we ignore Asia and move on to greener pastures, but I am suggesting that we don't favor Asia to the exclusion of several other attractive and progressive countries that might one day be "the new Asia."

During one of my recent visits I met a businessman in Italy. With his expanding sales efforts his business is growing in excess of 20% during the past year. Competition from South Africa has driven prices down and he is looking to create a new factory in Georgia, located along Russia's southern border and finally given its independence by that country in mid-1992. Georgia, he believes, offers a great opportunity for his products as well as lowering his manufacturing costs. (Sound like a familiar refrain?)

I have been so busy with China lately that I never thought about Georgia. It's not that I am going to rush out and change everything because of an inside tip. But I am sure going to look into other market places for my products and services.

My word of caution is to NOT ignore other countries. It is to INCLUDE the GLOBAL picture when considering markets and business opportunities. It is to UNDERSTAND that the global market is DYNAMIC. (By the way, it's about doing something about it as well.)

Yes, a lot of businesses are focused on China these days; and that's no accident. There are a lot of opportunities for the global entrepreneur in China, but we must keep our eye on the WHOLE picture. China is but a piece of the pie, a big piece, granted, but there are plenty of other slices for us to taste and, who knows, tempt our palate.

A few years ago I was working on a project that involved three different countries; The United States, China and Russia. Each had its own part in the manufacturing process, and each contributed in a unique and significant way. If we had just kept our eyes on China and not looked anywhere else for solutions to our needs, we would not have been able to find a solution for this customer.

Asia (and specifically China) is only one part of the global community. We've thought of China as one slice of the pie; now consider the global market as a jigsaw puzzle. If we just look at one piece, be it a pie or a puzzle, we can miss greater opportunities by burying our heads in the sand.

All of this sounds logical and rather fundamental, I know. But sometimes it takes plain language to share a plain concept. Forgive me if I'm overstating, but I have seen too many people make decisions that turned into business failures that could have been avoided if their eyes were open, even if they just looked at the neighboring country.

Let's take a company I knew who was just entering into China, for example: The American company in question was excited about the cost savings and the potential of selling their products inside of China.

The market was promising to double their business within a very short period of time. The cost of entering the market was small and everything seemed to be pointing toward success. After much deliberation, they began their journey. Within a year, their factory was up and running. Sales orders began to show promising signs of the expected growth.

Disaster hit, however, when an Indian company entered the Chinese market and undercut the American company by OVER 50%. Price wasn't the only factor that spelled the Americans' doom; their quality was excellent and the service was flawless.

Within the following 12 months, the American company pulled out of China and now holds a small market segment in the USA. The loss was staggering but they eventually regained their footing after many layoffs and other cost cutting measures.

The interesting aspect of this story is that it could have been avoided altogether. The Indian company was a popular supplier in Europe and was expanding into the Chinese market. The American company was so caught up in the market size of China that they didn't see a smaller Indian company coming up behind them and, as a result, got clipped.

The lesson to be learned here is that when it comes to what is best for your company, you cannot just consider one country. When you hired your latest employee, you didn't just interview one prospect, did you? When you bought your last house, you looked at several, if not more, right? So why shortchange your company's future? This is a GLOBAL market and we must consider the WHOLE picture when making a decision to expand across our boarders.

Remember: When all is said and done, when the hype dies down and the dust settles and you're left with basic business decisions, Asia is just one part of the world. Important as it is, we must still be diligent and step back once in a while to view the global picture to make the best decisions for our company.

PARTING WORDS

So, in the end, what does your future hold for you? And why am I qualified to predict YOUR future? Well, my company is probably a lot like yours and I've already come across a lot of the decisions, emotions, and questions you're experiencing right now.

That said, I do believe that *all* businesses in this country will face China during their life time and will ask themselves questions centered around either selling their product inside of China or producing (or sourcing) their product (s) from China. I am sure, if we look for the tag that say "made in China," we will find that we are already either competing with the product – or selling them.

China is booming. As we have seen, simply getting into the game can be both rewarding and frustrating, not to mention working, earning, and growing in a foreign market. How you go about getting the necessary information to make sound decisions will be critical to your success.

My personal journey throughout Asia has been a rewarding experience in my life, both personally and professionally. These pages represent but a few of my experiences, ones that I hope may have some benefit to the reader. Learning from others has its benefits, true enough, but the most lasting experiences are the ones that we have ourselves. I hope I have stimulated you into taking action with your own business, department, project or perhaps simply your own personal growth.

See you in China ...

Appendix:

Recommended Reading for the Entrepreneur in Asia

I've made reference in this book to the importance of "doing your homework." As we all know, no matter how great the Internet may seem or how trustworthy a friend's advice might be, all homework starts with one thing: A good book.

Part of my reason for writing this book was because so many people asked me to. They knew I'd been there, done that, and wanted me to put my experiences down so they could learn from them. But this book is just a part of the large library devoted to companies doing business in Asia.

Here, then, are some of the best:

China Briefing: The Practical Guide of China Business by Dezan Shira (**China Group**, 2003-2004)

> This should be required reading for every professional interested in conducting business in China. Not only do they publish a monthly magazine, but they have a very comprehensive book covering everything from History to Risk Management. Dezan Shira provides support on China Law, Tax Structuring, and Management for all types of companies. You can contact them on the Internet at: www.dezshira.com.

Kiss, Bow or Shake Hands by Terri Morrison, George A. Bordon and Wayne A. Conaway, 1994 (**B. Adams**, 1995)

> I think this is a book that everyone even considering doing business in another country needs to keep in their library. *Kiss, Bow or Shake Hands* provides you with the most current

information possible on what foreign business and social practices expect and/or demand. I always read this before I go on a trip, even though I have been in the country a hundred times. It keeps me tuned toward the proper practices of the country.

Managing Cultural Differences: Leadership Strategies for a New World of Business, Philip R. Harris and Robert T. Morgan (**Butterworth-Heinemann**, 2004)

I am not sure what edition they are on but this is a keeper even if you just happen across a used copy in the library clearance sale. It may be leaning toward an "academia" perspective but it really gives you a basis of awareness on cultural considerations. I would suggest reading it then read it again after six months of international business travel. It certainly will give you some shifting in how you view Management and Leadership in this new century.

International Management: Managing Across Borders and Cultures by Helen Deresky (**Prentice Hall**, 2003)

This globally oriented book covers the most current research and trends in International Management. It offers comprehensive and integrative cases that illustrate the actual behaviors and functions required for successful cross-cultural management at the strategic and interpersonal level. Includes numerous boxed features that relate concepts to real-world practice. Also includes experiential exercises for self-test. For professionals in international business.

International Business: Environments and Operations by John D. Daniels (**Prentice Hall**, 2003)

This classic bestseller discusses the differences faced in international environments, the overall strategies companies can take, and practical alternatives for operating abroad. Its abundance of colorful maps, strong engaging and opening cases, and classic and contemporary examples provide a balanced approach to all functions of business.

International Management: *Culture, Strategy, and Behavior with World Map* by Richard M Hodgetts, Fred Luthans (**McGraw-Hill**, 2002)

As a discipline of academy inquiry, International Management applies management concepts and techniques to their contexts in firms working in multinational, multicultural environments. Its 5th edition continues to set the standard for International Management texts with its research-based content and its balance between culture, strategy, and behavior.

International Business: *A Managerial Perspective* by Ricky W. Griffin, Mike W. Pustay (**Prentice Hall**, 2003)

This comprehensive overview of international business is divided into various business functions, making it clear and easy to understand. In every chapter "Culture Quest Insights" into culture, geography, and business lead readers to a multimedia experience of a certain country or region that provides useful information on the impact of culture on business.

Business Ethics: *A Global and Managerial Perspective* by David J Fritzsche (**McGraw-Hill**, 2004)

Fritzsche's: Business Ethics: A Global and Managerial Perspective 2e, integrates sociological theories and codes of morale that a manager might face in the modern business world. This paperback combines research and theory with real world examples and cases, discussion questions, and interactive "what would you do" situations.

INDEX

Sole Ownership, 201
Special Economic Zone, 36
standard of living, 106
Sun Tzu, 27
supply chain, 4, 5, 10, 13, 14,
   15, 205

T

taxes, 194, 195
Technology, 11, 12, 13, 15, 43,
   50, 55, 66, 74, 106, 117,
   151, 152, 198
teleconferencing, 116, 117
The Art of War, 27
trade deficit, 46
Transfer Pricing, 64

U

V

Value Added Tax, 65, 70, 71

W

Wal-Mart, 45, 117
Wen Jiabao, 39
Wholly Foreign Owned
   Enterprises, 54, 55, 192
World Trade Organization, 184,
   199
WTO, 8, 9, 46, 47, 74, 194

X

Xian, 34, 38

Z

Zhu Ronji, 39

www.ingramcontent.com/pod-product-compliance
Lightning Source LLC
Chambersburg PA
CBHW060546200326
41521CB00007B/505